Project No. 65 - P

THEN AND THERE SERIES

GENERAL EDITOR

MARJORIE REEVES, M.A., PH.D.

Scotland in the time of Wallace and Bruce

WILLIAM K. RITCHIE, M.A.

Illustrated from contemporary sources

LONGMAN

LONGMAN GROUP LIMITED
London

*Associated companies, branches and representatives
throughout the world*

© Longman Group Ltd 1970

First published 1970
Third impression 1973

ISBN 0 582 20461 5

*Printed in Hong Kong by
Dai Nippon Printing Co (International) Ltd*

FOR GRAEME

ACKNOWLEDGEMENTS

The author would like to thank the staffs of the National Library of Scotland, the
Scottish National Museum of Antiquities and the Scottish Record Office for their
willing assistance, and for reading his work in manuscript and offering helpful
criticism E. J. Simpson M.A., F.S.A.(Scot) and A. M. Stewart, M.A.
For permission to reproduce photographs we are grateful to the following:
Aberdeen Photographic Service, page 57; Arbroath Herald page 54; British
Museum, pages 1, 5 *(right)*, 8 *(top* and *bottom)*, 10 *(top* and *bottom)*, 12, 17 *(left,
top* and *bottom)*, 25 *(left* and *right)*, 29, 35, 38 *(bottom)*, 39 *(left* and *right)*, 40, 42–43
and 61; Bodleian Library, Oxford, pages 5 *(left)* and 20; Corporation of City of
Aberdeen, page 24; Controller of Her Majesty's Stationery Office and the Keeper
of the Records of Scotland (Crown Copyright Reserved) page 85; VAFirshoff,
page 69 *(bottom)*; Giraudon, page 37 *(left)*; George Hay, page 16 *(left)*; Francis
C. Inglis, Edinburgh, page 75; Wernher Kissling, page 8 *(middle)*; Ministry of
Public Building and Works, pages 31, 51 and 87; National Museum of Antiquities
of Scotland, pages 14, 16 *(right)*, 27, 38 *(top)*, and 42 *(top left* and *right)*; National
Trust for Scotland, page 19 *(bottom)*; C. d'O Pilkington Jackson, page 69 *(top)*;
Radio Times Hulton Picture Library, page 80; Science Museum London, (Crown
Copyright Reserved), page 48; Scottish Record Office, page 23, and also His Grace
the Duke of Buccleuch and Queensberry, page 45; the Pierpont Morgan Library
M.638, folios 20, 37v and 27v pages 33, 41 and 76; Westminster Abbey page 72.
The photograph on page 21 is reproduced by kind permission of the Hunterian
Museum, Glasgow and of the publishers, from Stewart, *The Scottish Coinage*,
Spink and Son; and the illustration on page 13 is redrawn from Symon *Scottish
Farming* © Oliver and Boyd by kind permission of the publishers.

Contents

To the Reader

Monday, 18 March 1286. All day long the storm raged. Savage northerly winds bringing rain and snow lashed the south of Scotland. The end of the world must be near, people said as they cowered indoors, shuddering with cold and fear. They trembled in the King's castle at Edinburgh. The King himself was there that day with his lords, discussing matters of state. In the afternoon, with discussion over, they broke off for dinner. It was a cheerless meal for all except the King. He at least was in high spirits. Then he rose to go. The rest of the company could not believe their ears. What! Go out in such a storm? Surely the King would not be so foolish! In vain they pleaded with him to stay. But storm or no storm, King Alexander was determined to join his young wife, Queen Yolande, at Kinghorn, on the other side of the Firth of Forth.

Off the King rode to the Ferry with only three squires for company. At Dalmeny the ferry-man begged him not to risk crossing the two miles of raging sea. Alexander insisted. By the time they reached the other side darkness had fallen. At Inverkeithing a local man offered him a bed for the night but Alexander pressed on along the track by the coast.

Exactly what happened next no one will ever know. In the morning they found the King on the beach not far from Kinghorn, dead with a broken neck. His horse had probably stumbled and thrown him. A long and happy reign was over.

This book tries to describe what Scotland was like during these years and those that came after his death. It tells how the Scottish people lived. You will see them at peace and at war. You will learn how they lost their freedom and how they won it back. So this book is also about their great leaders in this fight for freedom, William Wallace and Robert Bruce.

Words printed in *italics* are explained in the Glossary (p. 90)

1 The Land and the People

Can you recognise this map? It is a map of Scotland that was drawn in the thirteenth century. The names of a few districts, towns and islands are not very clearly written and you probably think that the shape and size are all wrong compared with the maps that you know. This is how a map-maker of the thirteenth century saw Scotland, but his map does not tell us a great deal about Scotland. If you look at the map inside the front cover of the book you may get a better idea of what the country was like. Use it to find the places mentioned in the book.

You will see that the boundaries of Scotland were almost the same as they are today. Notice that Orkney and Shetland are not shown. Lying to the north of Scotland, these islands still belonged to the King of Norway—as they would continue to do until 1472. The Isle of Man was part of Scotland and so too was Berwick-upon-Tweed.

When you look at this map of Scotland you must remember that the countryside was vastly different in many places from what it is today. Picture for yourself hillsides covered with dense forests of oak and pine, full of wolves and other wild

How a mapmaker in the thirteenth century drew Scotland

1

animals, and river valleys filled with marshes and small lochs. Here and there on the drier slopes of the valleys and in clearings in the forests lived small groups of people. Rough tracks criss-crossed the land, linking the places where the people lived, leading to fords and ferrying-places across rivers and lochs, and winding through the glens and passes of the Highlands. Separated by mountains, forests, lochs and rivers, the people lived in large families: in some places everybody was closely related to each other. They did not travel much and often knew little about what was happening in the world outside their own district.

It has been estimated that there were only about 400,000 people living in Scotland at this time. England had about five times that number. These Scots were a mixed lot, speaking several different languages. Most of them probably spoke Gaelic, in the centre and west as well as in the north. In the east, especially in Lothian, the language most commonly heard was 'Inglis', the same English that was spoken in the north of England. In the *burghs* along the east coast a few people would probably still be speaking the Flemish their ancestors had spoken, back in the Low Countries in what we call Belgium. In the far north and over in the Hebrides Norwegian would not have died out. All these were the languages of the common people. The King and his nobles spoke French.

Four centuries earlier there had not even been a kingdom of Scotland but several separate kingdoms, as you will see on this map. In the north and centre were the Picts in ancient Alba; stretching south-westwards from the mouth of the River Clyde were the Britons in Strathclyde; over in the south-east were the Angles of Lothian in what had been part of the English kingdom of Northumbria, while in what is now Argyll were the Scots of Dalriada. By 1034 these kingdoms had been brought together under one ruler, a descendant of the royal family of the Scots.

In the meanwhile Norsemen had settled round the northern and western edges of Scotland, on the mainland as well as in

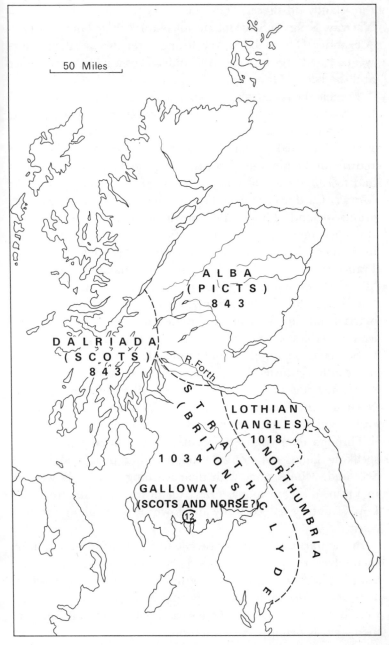

50 Miles

ALBA
(PICTS)
8 4 3

DALRIADA
(SCOTS)
8 4 3

R. Forth

STRATHCLYDE
(BRITONS)

LOTHIAN
(ANGLES)
1018

NORTHUMBRIA

1 0 3 4

GALLOWAY
(SCOTS AND NORSE ?)
12

the islands off-shore. They owed allegiance to the kings of Norway. Kings of Scots fought to conquer these lands. In 1249 Alexander II won back Argyll and after defeating the Norwegians at Largs in 1263, Alexander III gained the Hebrides and the Isle of Man.

French speaking people came to Scotland after 1066 and the Norman Conquest of England. Scottish kings, who had been educated at the court of the new Norman kings of England invited Norman knights to come to Scotland. In return for helping the Scottish kings to fight their enemies and to rule over wild outlying parts of their country such as Moray, Caithness and Galloway, they were given generous grants of land. They settled down in Scotland though they still spent much of their time on their estates in England and in France. They were usually called after their homes in France and so they had 'de' before their name; for example, 'de Brus', 'de Bailleul'. Through time they became known as 'the Bruce', 'the Balliol', or plain 'Bruce' and 'Balliol'. Many married into noble Scottish families and rose to become the leading nobles of the land. These Normans brought new ideas to Scotland, so rapid changes took place in the twelfth and thirteenth centuries in law, land-holding and government. These new ideas are described as 'feudal' and we say that the Normans introduced *feudalism* into Scotland. The ancient customs of Scotland, however, did not die out.

Through their connections with the Continent the French-speaking kings and nobles brought other people to live in Scotland. Monks came with their learning and books written in Latin to set up monasteries; Flemish merchants from the Low Countries helped trade and towns to grow along the east coast.

In the thirteenth century people in Scotland still thought of themselves as belonging to a particular family, district or burgh. They were only just beginning to think of themselves as Scots, in the same way as people in France and England were beginning to see themselves as Frenchmen and Englishmen, that is being part of a nation.

Scotland was a small country and not very rich, yet it produced two of the most remarkable men of the thirteenth century. Both of them were better known abroad than at home. John Duns Scotus was called 'the subtle doctor' because he was such a clever and learned teacher. He got his name from Duns in Berwickshire, where he is thought to have been born in 1265. After attending the universities of Cambridge, Oxford and Paris he became famous as one of the deepest thinkers of his time. Those who passed on his ideas became known as Scotists or Dunses. Centuries later they were jeered at for clinging to these ideas when other scholars said they were out-of-date. This is how the word 'dunce' came into being.

Michael Scot came from the Border country too. He was born about 1175 somewhere near the head-waters of the Tweed, it is said. He studied mathematics, *theology*, law and medicine. There were no universities in Scotland in those days so, like Duns Scotus, he had to study in England and France. He went even farther, to Spain and Italy. He became the tutor and later the friend of the Emperor Frederick II, ruler of Germany and parts of Italy and well known for his great interest in learning as 'Wonder of the World'. Michael Scot translated the books of great philosophers from Arabic into Latin, the language that all scholars then used. He also

Michael Scot, the 'wizard'

Students with their teacher at university

taught at the famous medical school at Salerno in Italy. A book that he wrote on medicine was read by medical students for centuries afterwards. Like other learned men of his time Michael Scot dabbled in *astrology*. He was said to be a conjurer, a magician and a seer into the future. Back in the Borders, where he died in 1232, many wonderful stories were told about his supernatural powers, and for centuries he has been known as Michael Scot, the 'Wizard'.

2 Living in the Countryside

Most people in the thirteenth century were farmers. They produced nearly all their own food, made clothes for themselves and even built their own houses. In Scotland they lived together in small groups of families, between four and ten, with their land round about, in what were called 'farm touns'. Where there was plenty of land for farming, the touns could be as large as 104 Scots acres, but the size of the touns varied a good deal throughout the country.

AT WORK

If we took a close look at one such toun we would see that the land the farmers cultivated was a lot of long patches of ground without fences or walls, sprawling up and down the hillsides, with the earth in each patch piled high in the middle. We would notice that these patches were divided into ridges or strips, known as 'rigs'. Each rig was between 20 and 40 feet wide and perhaps about 200 yards long. These rigs were the farmers' land. One farmer might have as many as thirty rigs, not lying all together, but scattered among those of his neighbours in the toun, and separated from one another by low-lying stretches of waste-ground known as 'baulks'. Every year or so the farmers changed round their rigs. In this way everyone was sure to receive some of the good as well as some of the poorer land. All this land round about was called the infield, and the name given to this kind of farming is run-rig.

For about five or six years the farmers would cultivate their infield and then they allowed it to rest for a year or two to let the goodness come back to the soil. Meanwhile they ploughed up the poorer ground beyond the infield and grew crops on what they called the outfield. In most years this was used for grazing sheep, goats and cattle.

Above: *Ploughing. Where the soil was heavier more oxen were needed*

Left: *A crofter in the twentieth century using a cas-chrom*

Below: *Harrowing. What is the man on the left doing?*

The crops the farmers grew most were oats and a rough kind of barley known as bere. They grew some peas and beans also. Only in the sheltered parts of the country, along the east coast in the Merse, the Mearns and the Laigh of Moray, was it dry and warm enough to grow much wheat.

The farmers all worked together in the toun. In spring they yoked their oxen together to form a team to pull the wooden plough. Sometimes the plough was so heavy that eight or ten oxen were needed to pull it. Four men were required, one to steer the plough, another at the front to guide the oxen, with the other two walking on either side, ready to steady the plough or goad the animals. Work could be very slow. There were many breakdowns. The oxen often stumbled, the plough got stuck in heavy soil or the *coulter* broke. By the end of the day they might have ploughed only half an acre. Where the soil was very thin and stony a plough was useless and men broke up the soil with a hand-plough or cas-chrom, as it is called in Gaelic.

There was work to do all year round. After ploughing and as soon as the snows had cleared came sowing-time. Sometimes this was held up till April. With birds swarming and circling about, the farmers would walk up and down the furrows in their rigs, casting handfuls of seed from a box at their waist. Next came harrowing to press the seeds into the ground. Then, if God was kind, there would be enough sunshine and not too much rain so that everyone could look forward to a good harvest.

Everybody helped to get in the crops: boys and girls, old folks and young, women as well as the men, night and day, reaping the corn with their *sickles* and setting it up in *stooks*. Then came threshing with their *flails* and winnowing to separate the husks from the grain, by throwing up handfuls into the air to let the wind blow away the chaff. The grain left on the ground was then scooped up to be made into meal, either at the mill by the river or in the *quern* at home.

A farmer might have only one ox, a cow, a few sheep, some pigs and poultry. Compared with ours the animals would be

9

Above: *Harvest*
Below: *Threshing with flails*

small and scraggy. They grazed on the hillsides or nibbled on the outfield in spring and summer. In winter they were often kept indoors, surviving on a diet of boiled chaff, whins and straw. Oxen were fed more than cows to make them strong enough to pull the plough. Many beasts were killed off in autumn because food was so scarce for them during the winter. The *carcases* were preserved in *brine*; they were called 'marts' from Martinmas, the time of the year in November when the animals were slaughtered.

The farmers did not own the land they *tilled*. It belonged to the laird or landlord, and they had to pay him rent as his tenants. This rent was not usually paid in cash but in food—

10

so many chickens or so much meal, for example. They had also to work on the laird's own farm known as the mains farm. Harvest time was when they were most useful to him. Sometimes the landlord was not a person but an abbey. Monasteries owned a great deal of land and the monks were very keen farmers. In a book kept at the Abbey of Kelso were listed the duties that tenants on the abbey's estates were expected to perform. Here are some of these duties:

    4 days' reaping in harvest by all the family
    1 day's reaping by the farmer and two men
    1 day's carting *peats*
    ploughing $1\frac{1}{2}$ acres
    1 day's harrowing
    1 day with wagon in harvest
    1 man for sheep-washing
    1 man and horse to Berwick once a year with load of 3 *bolls* of corn or 2 bolls of salt or $1\frac{1}{2}$ bolls of coal
    carriage of the Abbot's wool to the Abbey and carrying goods across the moor to Lesmahagow.

In addition they had to pay the Abbey 6s 8d in cash every year. By 1300 these tenants were paying a rent of 11s instead of doing all these tasks.

Many people who worked on the land were not free to work where they wanted. They were serfs, which means that they belonged to their landlord as if they were his property. Here is part of a document in which we see a nobleman giving people to an abbey, in the same way as he grants land.

    'Know ye all that I have given [and] granted to the abbot and *convent* of Inchaffray in pure and perpetual *alms*, John, called Starnes, son of Thomas, son of Thora, with all his children; and for me and my heirs for ever I grant to the said abbot and convent all right and claim which I have or which I or my heirs may have in future on the said John or his offspring.'

Many serfs bought their freedom from their lords, and so after the thirteenth century there were few serfs in Scotland except in salt-making and coal-mining.

If the harvest was good the people did not starve. They had two meals a day: dinner about midday and supper in the evening when work was done. Their food was very simple and mostly home-produced. They ate much porridge and *bannocks* made of oatmeal, as well as cheese. For refreshment they drank ale that they brewed from barley. Peas and beans and *kail* were added to stock to make a thick soup called brose. Chickens and eggs were plentiful and so were river salmon, loch trout, herrings and other sea-fish. In the forests deer, rabbits and game were hunted. There was not much beef and mutton to eat; besides, meat was very stringy and tasteless, and spices to give it flavour were expensive. Sugar was dear too, but many people kept bees for their honey.

In many homes there was a loom for weaving cloth. Women spun the wool by hand and made it into a rough greyish-brown cloth. Leather from their cattle's hide might be tanned at home too, and made into shoes and hoods. From the flax they grew women made their own linen. The cut of their clothes was very plain. Styles for the dress of ordinary people seem to have remained unchanged for centuries. Men and boys wore a woollen tunic tied at the waist with a belt, and a pair of long *hose* strapped with straw leggings. They had no pockets in their hose, but they had a leather pouch hanging from their belt. Over their head and shoulders they sometimes wore a hood. Their shoes were made of soft leather and turned up at the toe. Boys and girls often went barefoot, and so did grown-ups when they were working. The clothes of women and girls were just as simple and not much different from what men wore: an ankle-length frock, hitched up at the

A woman at her spinning-wheel

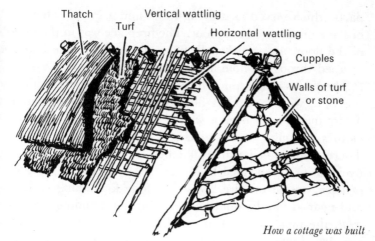

Labels on the illustration:

Thatch
Turf
Vertical wattling
Horizontal wattling
Cupples
Walls of turf or stone

How a cottage was built

waist, when working, over a linen under-slip. On her head a woman wore a *cowl* of wool or linen.

Men and women both wore their hair long, and most men seem to have had short rough beards.

AT HOME

The houses in the touns were so low-built that it must have been hard for a stranger to see them from a distance. They were made from materials that were easy to come by: wood, stone, turf and thatch.

First of all a framework was made consisting of three, four or five pairs of tree-trunks. Each pair was sunk firmly into the ground, tied together at the top and fixed by means of wooden pegs to a ridge-pole running along the pairs of tree-trunks. Stones were piled up to make the walls, with *divots* stuffed into the spaces between the stones. A layer of clay or mud was added. Over the wooden framework thin strong branches were woven and pinned down, then covered with turf. On some houses a thatch roof was laid on top of that. To keep the roof from blowing away, heavy stones were slung over it, tied to ropes made of straw. There were no windows and a piece of leather stretched over a wooden frame covered the doorway.

The house was divided by a low wall or fencing into two 13

parts which served as a living-room and a *byre*. Beaten earth or flat stones served as a floor. The fireplace was in the middle of the floor, an open hearth from which the smoke rose and escaped through a hole in the roof.

There was never much furniture. Box-beds were built into the wall, with mattresses filled with straw, ferns or heather. There might have been a *kist* for keeping any spare sheets or clothes, a rough trestle-table and a few three-legged stools. There would not be many kitchen utensils either. Swinging over the fire suspended from the rafters would be a big iron *cauldron*, beside the fire lay a flat stone for baking bannocks and near at hand would be the quern for grinding corn into *meal*, the meal-kist and an earthenware pot for keeping the salt dry. Lying about would be a water-bucket, a milk-pail

14

A stone quern for grinding corn

and cheese-press. People ate out of bowls made of earthenware or wood, and supped with horn spoons. Farm tools would be scattered about here and in the byre. Outside there might be a sledge for dragging home peats to burn. These were stacked for winter and when the supply was all burned people had to go out and dig more.

Not much of a house you might say. Imagine having to share the same roof with oxen. Yet this was home for most people at this time, or rather a shelter for the night. Most of the day, as long as it was light, they were out at work. If enemies came and burned their house down it did not take long to build it up again.

Though life could be hard, with long winters, wet summers, poor harvests and disease among the livestock, people enjoyed themselves too. When work was done they would gather round the fire and sing songs and tell stories. Some of these stories have been handed down in *ballads* and folk-tales. You may like to read some for yourself one day. They are full of adventures of ancient heroes, giants and the 'wee folk', who were firmly believed to play all kinds of tricks on ordinary people. There was always the local burgh to visit on market-day and the annual fair to look forward to. Though they did not have holidays as we have, there were many holy days of the Church when no work was to be done.

GOING TO CHURCH

On holy days and every Sunday people went to their kirk, their local parish church. It was a humble little building, not much bigger than a cottage in some parishes, but with white-washed walls. There the congregation would sit on the stools they had brought with them or else just stand about. The service was quite short. They would watch and listen as the priest performed the mysterious ceremony of the *Mass*. Much of the service they did not understand because the priest chanted the prayers in Latin. They came to the church for more besides the service. They were married by the priest at the church door and he baptised their children at the font   15

Left: *This is inside Dalmeny Church, West Lothian, today. It dates back to the twelfth century but there would have been no chairs then. Notice the Norman arch*
Below: *A candlestick, that may have been used in a church*

inside. Here they might come for *sanctuary* if they were accused of committing some crime, and be safe for up to forty days from being dragged away. The church was where local people held meetings. Time and again they had to be prevented from using it as a dance-hall!

The priest was a simple man like themselves, having only a little more learning than most men. He lived alongside his people in his *manse* and worked in his share of the toun's rigs. This was called his glebe. The church forbade priests to marry but he was looked after by a house-keeper. Parishioners also brought him their teinds–a tithe or tenth of what they earned. This was usually in the form of food. They paid him for baptisms, weddings and funerals also. When they died he prayed for their souls and buried their bodies in the churchyard.

The priest was appointed by the laird, or as we should say, presented by the laird to his living. It was the bishop, how-

Above: *an eighteenth-century engraving of Glasgow Cathedral*

Above left: *a priest at Mass*

Below left: *here is a Bishop. Notice his ring and staff and the mitre on his head*

ever, who was supposed to see that he did his job properly. A bishop looked after all the priests in the parishes of his *diocese*. There were eleven bishops in Scotland, the chief ones being the Bishops of St Andrews and Glasgow. Scotland had no archbishops like other countries until the fifteenth century. Bishops were very important men. They were appointed by the Pope, but the King had a say in who were to be chosen, which was just as well. They did all kinds of work for kings and popes: they acted as advisers, ambassadors and even as commanders in the army! Services in their church (called a cathedral) were carried out by other clergymen known as the dean and chapter.

17

3 Living in a Burgh

Suppose we found ourselves one morning in the company of some country folk. Some would be leading a cow or a few sheep, others walking alongside mules with *panniers* on their backs or driving carts pulled by oxen. Women would be carrying baskets full of eggs and cheese and panniers and carts would be laden with corn, hides and skins or bales of wool. We would know that they were on their way to market in the nearby burgh.

A burgh was a town that stood beside a castle. It consisted of rows of houses with plots of ground behind, surrounded by a stout wooden *palisade* and a deep ditch. Outside the burgh the townsfolk grazed their cattle on the burgh *muir* and grew their oats and barley in the town's acres. These people were farmers but they had other work to do as well, as we shall see.

The only way into a burgh was through one of the few ports or gateways, that were carefully guarded to keep out unwelcome strangers. A gate-keeper stood watch and collected *tolls* from visitors bringing goods to sell inside. At night he closed the gate. Each port had a name, such as the Sand Port or the West Port.

There was only one street in a burgh, the High Gate or High Street. Running off it were tiny lanes, known as wynds. Only the High Street was laid with cobbles. There were no pavements, however: everyone tried to walk in the middle of the street, the 'croun o' the *causey*', to avoid the middens or piles of rubbish, heaped in front of the houses, that were cleared away on Sunday morning.

The houses stood with their gable-ends facing the High Street. They were just like country cottages, though some had two storeys with outside stairs. A few were decorated with carved corner posts and covered with a white or coloured wash. Behind each house was a long narrow piece of enclosed

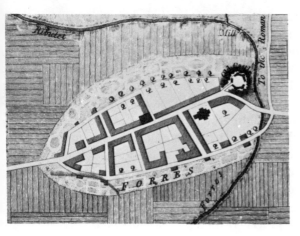

A plan of Forres, drawn in the early nineteenth century

*A market cross, from Culross in Fife Except for the plinth this is quite
new. The houses in the background date from the Seventeenth century.*

ground, stretching as far as the edge of the burgh. This was the townsman's *toft,* where he kept his byres, stables and sheds and where he might grow some peas, beans and kail.

About half-way along the High Street opened out. We would know from the houses that this was where the richest people lived. On one side would be the burgh kirk, in some burghs the only building made of stone. In the middle of the street stood the Cross. In former times it was to show that the people were Christian. Now it marked the town centre. Here people came to listen to travelling preachers, the friars, dressed in their rough habits of grey or black and therefore known as the Greyfriars and the Blackfriars. Here too they would laugh and jeer at unhappy law-breakers, sitting in the 'kuk-stool' or ducking-stool. This is where they came when they heard the town drum sounding to listen to some announcement being made. And, of course, this is where the weekly market was held.

Market-day was the busiest day in the week. In the early morning men were busy putting up stalls in the street. Soon they were full of things to sell that the burgh-folk had made: saddles, pots, bales of cloth and piles of shoes. Soon the country-folk would come with their goods for sale and buy what they did not produce themselves. They might take home a load of salt, for instance, or a new coulter for their plough. Some people in the burgh spent most of their time making things to sell and did not have time to grow food for themselves and so they might buy food in the market.

20

A friar preaching

Scottish coins from the thirteenth century were this size

There were many rules for trading in the burgh to make sure that no one was cheated. People could buy and sell only in the market-place. Goods had to be clearly displayed. Prices were fixed so that no trader could charge high prices and make a huge profit or charge low ones and so take trade away from others. Here are some prices charged around this time: a cow cost 4s 5d, a sheep cost 10d and a *chalder* of oatmeal cost £1. All goods had to be weighed at the public weight, or Tron.

Throughout the day money would change hands fast. Here are the only Scottish coins that were minted at this time. They were pennies, halfpennies and farthings made of silver. Dunbar and Inverness were two of the many burghs where they were minted.

There were no standard weights and measures for the whole country. People used local ones, such as the Stirling pint and the Edinburgh *ell*. An inch was reckoned to be equal in length to three grains of barley laid end to end.

Buying and selling was the main occupation of people in the burgh. That is why it was surrounded by a fence or wall, so that people could trade in peace under the protection of the castle beside it. Most burghs belonged to the King because they were built on his land. Some belonged to a nobleman, such as Prestwick and Annan, others, like Dunfermline and Glasgow, belonged to the Church. All tenants had to pay rent to their landlord. By this time they paid rent in money, though earlier they had had to help to guard the local castle. In the King's burghs rents were paid to the King's sheriffs, who lived in the royal castles. This rent amounted to 5d a year for every 200 feet of house frontage a person might have in the burgh.

The burghs brought in a lot of money for the King. Besides collecting the rents the sheriffs gathered in also the tolls charged on incomers to the burgh, customs duties on goods exported and taxes on things sold in the market. Here are some of these charges: for bringing into the burgh a *wain* of four oxen, 4d; on the sale of a chalder of corn or salt, 1d, an ox, $\frac{1}{2}d$, a thousand herring, 1d. The burghs were useful to the King in another way too. They were outposts of law and order in the far north and west, where little attention was paid to the King's orders.

Because the burghs were important to the King for bringing in wealth and keeping order, the King granted privileges to the burgh merchants. They were the only people who were allowed to trade in the country's most valuable products, skins, hides and wool. Only they could trade with foreign merchants. During the thirteenth century the burghs were becoming rich. The merchants of many burghs were beginning to pay their rents to the King in the form of an annual rent from the whole burgh, called a 'feu-ferme', instead of each townsman paying him separately. This pleased the King because he knew that he could count on a fixed sum of money coming in from each burgh every year and it was easy to collect.

Burgh-folk were very proud of their rights and privileges. These were all written down on a document made of parchment and bearing the King's own seal and the names of witnesses. It was called the burgh charter and was much prized. (See the next page.) Burgh-folk were free men. Serfs who wanted to escape from their lords could become free men provided they could pay the King rent and survive 'for a year and a day' in one of his burghs. Many became free in this way and the

22

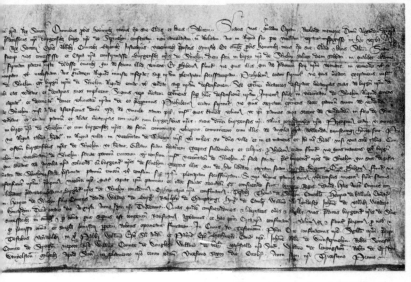

Above: *the charter of Stirling*

number of people living in the burghs rose.

The biggest and wealthiest Scottish burgh was Berwick. In 1296 it had about a thousand inhabitants and covered about 40 acres. The customs duties collected there in one year were estimated to be worth £2,190. A little later the feu-ferme for the burgh was fixed at £333 6s 8d. One writer at the time said that Berwick was as rich as ancient Alexandria in Egypt, though this was certainly an exaggeration. Around this time it was bigger than Edinburgh, Stirling, Aberdeen and Perth which had only a few hundred inhabitants and which were poor in comparison to Berwick.

BURGH COUNCIL AND BURGH COURT

By the end of the thirteenth century some burghs were beginning to be run not by the King but by a burgh council. It was elected by the leading men, who were called burgesses. Elections took place every year at Michaelmas, at the end of September. Meetings sometimes took place in the burgh kirk. There the council passed laws for the burgh which all had to observe. These and any other documents belonging to the

23

council would be signed with the burgh seal. Here is the seal of Aberdeen. The council consisted of about a dozen men, of whom the provost, as he came to be called, was the chief. He was assisted by the *bailies*. They collected money that had to be paid to the sheriff and also acted as judges in the burgh court, trying offenders brought before them by armed men known as the burgh sergeants. The bailies could impose fines and also sentence criminals to death.

Sometimes disputes arose between merchants of different burghs. These were heard in the Court of the Four Burghs, which represented the four chief burghs, Berwick, Roxburgh, Edinburgh and Stirling. Through time this court grew until all burghs were members. Nowadays it is called the Convention of Royal Burghs which meets every year in Edinburgh.

THE GUILD

In most burghs the men who sat on the council were also members of the Merchant Guild. This was a very important body of men because they controlled all the trade in the burgh. It was they who made the regulations about the buying and selling that took place in the market. None but they might 'buy hides, wool or wool skins to sell again, nor cut cloth unless he be a brother of our Guild'. So ran another of these regulations passed by the members sitting in their Guildhall with their Alderman acting as chairman. Members

24

Right: a leper. Note the marks on his face and hand

Below: fish for sale

who broke the rules of the Guild were fined. Members of guilds from other burghs were allowed to trade in the burgh but only with merchants, not with the public. Anybody from another burgh was a 'foreigner'; he was allowed to spend only one night and his host had to be responsible for his good behaviour!

We can still read the laws of the guild of Berwick that were probably copied by the guilds of other burghs. They tell us that the guildsmen made laws for other matters beside trade, as this one shows:

> We *ordain* that no one dare to place filth or any dust or ashes on the common way, or in the market-place, or on the banks of the Tweed, to the hurt and damage of the passers-by. If anyone do so, he shall be fined eight shillings as forfeit.

Another law forbade lepers from coming into the burgh. They had to stay outside and were supposed to live as well as they could by themselves in leper colonies. Leprosy was a dreaded disease and could not be cured in those days.

Guild members were supposed to treat one another as brothers. If they quarrelled they could be fined 40 pence, if they carried a knife 'within the bounds of the Guild' the fine was 12 pence, and if they drew blood it was 20 shillings.

25

Members were to help one another: to supply a fellow member with goods to sell if he had run short; to support those who had fallen sick and take care of the widows and orphans. They were even expected to pay ransom for a member who was captured by pirates at sea.

CRAFTSMEN

Only merchants could be members of the Guild. Craftsmen were allowed to join only if they gave up working with their hands and employed others to do their work for them.

There were many craftsmen. Some worked at making cloth: the fullers, the dyers, the websters, for instance. There were the tailors who made up the finished cloth for the customers. Others worked in leather: the skinners, tanners and saddlers. There were also the millers, the bakers, the *fleshers* and many more. Through time the craftsmen were to form guilds of their own, one for each craft, to protect themselves against the richer and more powerful merchants and also to keep up standards of good workmanship.

You would find the craftsmen in their workshops down the wynds of the burgh, sometimes several of the same craft in the same wynd in a row. A painted sign above the workshop would tell of what went on below. A loaf might represent a baker and a pair of scissors a tailor. Passers-by could see into the workshop through an open window with no glass, that was covered with shutters at night. Inside worked the master craftsman with his journeyman and apprentices. A journeyman was paid about threepence a day. He lived with his master until he could afford to get married and set up house for himself. No doubt he longed for the day when he would be rich enough to be his own master with a shop of his own. First, however, he had to produce his 'master's piece' to prove to the other masters of his craft that he was skilled enough to become one of them. The apprentices were young boys still learning their craft. They were often beaten by their master for being lazy or mischievous. At night they slept under the counter in his workshop.

26

Merchants as well as craftsmen lived in a house above their place of business. Rich though a merchant might be, he might still have only one room. It was called his *solar* and he reached it from the street by an outside stair. It must have been very crowded because it served as kitchen, dining-room, bedroom and sitting-room. Here is a list of household goods that a burgess was expected to have:

1 best table with trestles
1 table-cloth
1 towel, basin, *laver*
1 best feather bed with sheets and bed-clothes
1 *gylfat*
1 barrel
1 cauldron, kettle, *brander*, brass pot, pan, roasting-iron, *girdle*
1 chimney
1 crook for hanging pot over the fire

1 *mortar and pestle*
1 *mazer*
1 *platter*
1 cup
12 spoons
1 bench, stool, form
1 balance and weights
1 *kist*
1 axe and spade
1 plough, wain, cart, waggon
1 *shearing-hook*

Though this seems too much for one small house, remember that the merchant had stables and sheds and a byre in his toft at the back.

A bronze pot. Why has it three feet?

27

If you thought that the burgh was busy on market-day you had not seen the burgh when the annual fair was on. Not every burgh had the privilege of holding one. In those that had, there was tremendous bustle and excitement. All normal business and the regulations that went with it stopped for a week and sometimes longer. A small town made of canvas booths grew up almost overnight outside the burgh. From far and near came merchants, many of them from overseas, with luxuries rarely seen at other times in Scotland: smooth, rich cloth from the Low Countries and Italy, fine soft leather from France and Spain that came with loads of salt and casks of wine and bundles of onions and garlic. From more distant lands still, Palestine, Persia and India, for example, were brought rare herbs and spices, dried fruits, nuts, rice, pepper and ginger, and expensive dye-stuffs, such as *madder* and *brazil-wood*. Scottish goods would be on sale, wool from the Border sheep and hides and skins from cattle and wild animals. Fish too was always in demand by merchants from the Continent.

At the fair all kinds of people mingled in the crowds. Townsmen rubbed shoulders with countrymen and soldiers from the castle mixed with monks from the monastery. Even the King might come and buy.

Fairs were a time for having good fun as well as for doing business. There were travelling jugglers to watch, acrobats and men with performing bears, minstrels, wrestlers and weird sooth-sayers with fortunes to tell. To those who got into trouble the law was lenient. Once 'the peace of the fair' was announced offenders were tried before a special court. It was called 'Piepowder Court', from 'pieds poudrés', the French for 'dusty-feet' or pedlars. There were plenty of these around, buying up trinkets and ribbons, combs and mirrors to sell on their travels.

Soon the fair was over for another year and people went back to work as usual. Work and play throughout the year, however, ended at nightfall. As shutters were put up in house and workshop, wynds and High Street became dark and deserted. No one went out at night, or was supposed to go out, except those on watch duty. All had to take turns at walking round the burgh at night, with lantern and spear, checking the ports and walls and watching for fire. Meanwhile the other burgh folk slept till daybreak and time to start another day.

Wrestlers

4 Living in a Castle

Castles were built to defend the country against invaders and protect the people from law-breakers. Those who lived in a castle were the King and his nobles, with their families and servants.

The oldest castles were called 'motte and bailey' castles and some were still standing in Scotland in the thirteenth century. They consisted of a wooden tower standing on top of a mound of earth (the motte), surrounded by a palisade and ditch, and connected by a wooden bridge to a low courtyard (the bailey) which also had a ditch and palisade. Many of the newer castles, however, were made of stone. They were larger and consisted of towers linked by high curtain walls.

On the next page is a castle that was built in the middle of the thirteenth century. This is Dirleton, in East Lothian, as it might have looked a little after this time. It was built on a rock that stood up sharply from the flat countryside round about. Notice its four round towers jutting out from the curtain walls. These walls were as thick as fifteen feet in places. The biggest tower was called the donjon. It measured 36 feet in diameter and its walls were ten feet thick.

The rock on which it was built and the thickness of its walls made Dirleton Castle very strong against attack. It was made even more secure in other ways still. Along the top of the towers and walls wooden galleries were built out over the deep moat or ditch on its south side. This was to enable defenders to fire arrows and throw stones and spears on the enemy who would be trying to dig away at the castle's foundations. The entrance was heavily guarded by a gate-house with two turrets and a drawbridge. There were also two *portcullises* and a pair of heavy wooden yetts, or doors, strengthened with iron. Over the narrow space between the two doors was a murder-hole, through which boiling water could be poured on attackers who had succeeded in penetrating as far.

For most of the thirteenth century Scotland was a peaceful country, so we should think of a castle as a huge house and not as a fortress always under siege. Dirleton was the home of the de Vaux, a local family who had built the castle around 1250. They had a few servants and tenants who would take their turn at standing guard, sleeping in the guard-room just inside the castle gate, but spending most of their time serving their master or working in the fields outside. The de Vaux family lived in the donjon. Their biggest apartment was the Chamber, or Hall, an upstairs room with six sides and a domed ceiling. There was a large open fire-place on one side and on four others were windows, set in deep recesses with stone benches for window seats. The windows were very

Dirleton Castle, as a modern artist thinks it may have looked in the fourteenth century

narrow and had iron bars and wooden shutters instead of glass. The walls may have been left bare or covered with whitewash. It is possible that they might have been covered with *wainscotting*, painted cloth or tapestry as they were in other castles. There would not be much furniture: one or two heavy high-backed chairs, a trestle table and a kist or two might have been all. The floor would be covered with rushes or plain straw. In some castles there might possibly be a rare carpet or rug that a crusader had brought back from Spain or Palestine.

The Chamber was a public room where the lord of the castle conducted business, received guests and where everyone had their meals. Dirleton was only a small castle; in some larger castles the hall was oblong and had a raised dais, and could accommodate many of the servants as well as the nobleman and his guests and family.

There were other small apartments. The chapel was where the chaplain said daily Mass. The wardrobe was a kind of store-room, not only for clothes but for anything of value, such as jewels, spare furniture and even expensive foodstuffs. The only private room in the castle was the solar, a kind of bed-sitting room. During the day the bed served as a couch. It was a four-poster, with linen hangings and a feather mattress that was slung across thongs of leather or cord. In the corners of the room were kists containing bed-linen. Sticking out from the wall were perches for hanging clothes. All rooms were draughty since they had no doors, only curtains. There were no bathrooms, and so when someone wanted a bath he had to sit in a deep tub in front of the fire. There were toilets, but they were little *alcoves* called garderobes, built into the outside walls, with long *chutes* that led down to the moat.

The castle courtyard, or close, was usually a busy place. This was where you would find the kitchen, the stables, the brewhouse, byre and bakehouse, all rough wooden shacks with lean-to roofs of thatch. Stores of grain and meat, the rents of the lord's tenants, were kept in the castle vaults under

the towers. At Dirleton the storerooms were gouged out of the rock. Down here too was the dark pit, where the lord could keep prisoners.

Many people beside the lord and his family lived in a castle. In the castle of a powerful baron there would always be many guests. He would have the sons of some neighbouring lords living with him and learning to be knights. They were called pages. At the age of five they would begin by learning how to ride and manage a horse, how to handle weapons and also

33

how to dance and behave in the company of ladies. At meal-times they would serve their master at table. By the age of fourteen a boy would be known as a squire. His training would now be more taken up with learning how to fight, and he would help his master to put on his armour. When he was a little older a young man was ready to become a knight.

There might be several young knights living in a large castle. Fortunately for the lady of the castle there were plenty of servants. A very powerful baron would entrust much of the work of running his estates to his steward, who had many other servants to help him. There was the seneschal, who looked after the Hall, the chamberlain who was in charge of the private quarters, and the butler and pantler who each saw to the supply of drink and food in the buttery and pantry. Under these higher servants would be clerks, cooks, bakers and many *scullions* and laundry-maids. This is not including the outdoor staff under the marischal, who looked after the wagons and horses, with his grooms, huntsmen, stableboys, the smith and the *farrier*. All had to be fed, clothed and paid. From the accounts kept by a steward in a great baronial household in England about this time we learn that a boy who worked in the bakehouse was paid 7s for two years' work, a clerk was paid $4\frac{1}{2}d$ a day, and a cook, a pantler and a tailor each earned 2d a day. Remember that their master paid for their food and lodging and their clothes too. A clerk's clothes were worth 30s and a cook's 9s.

HOW THEY DRESSED

The clothes that high-born people wore were longer, finer and more colourful than those worn by anyone else. They dressed in bright colours: reds, blues and purple. Their clothes reached to their ankles and their very best clothes were made of silk, which came from France and Italy. Most of the time, however, they wore wool and linen. Many of their outer garments were lined with fur, which was as well, because their homes were damp and draughty.

34   Clothes for men and women were simple in design. Both

wore a long-sleeved tunic, or cotte, as it is called, that was slit at the neck and hung in heavy folds from a girdle tied at the waist. A woman's sleeves were buttoned at the wrist and the man's hung loose. From a woman's belt dangled a bunch of keys or a purse, from a man's hung the sheath for his knife. Over their cotte men and women wore a short surcoat, either without sleeves or with ones that were long and wide. When they went out riding they put on a wide cloak that fastened at the neck with a brooch. Underneath their cotte men wore woollen breeches on top of long drawers, that were kept up with a cord like our modern pyjamas. Women wore a long *chemise*. Stockings were made of wool for women as well as for men. Shoes were of soft leather or felt, with no heel, slightly pointed and fastened at the ankle with a button. Out of doors calf-length boots with no heels were worn. When out riding all wore gloves, some of which were studded with jewels.

Ladies and gentlemen kept their hair long. It was nearly always covered, even indoors. A lady might be able to brush her hair down to the small of her back. During the day she usually coiled it up and kept it in place with pins under a white linen *wimple* that covered her neck as well as her head. Sometimes she wore a veil too. Young girls mostly went bare-headed and kept their hair tidy with a metal band or chaplet of flowers. Men's hair was cut in a fringe and reached the nape of the neck. They kept it in place with a close-fitting cap that tied under the chin and which was often gaily embroidered for young men.

A lady having her hair combed

Only when a lord went off to fight did he wear armour. Because it was so heavy and made up of several pieces it took him a long time to put it on. That is why he needed his squire to help him. Next to his shirt he wore a long-sleeved tunic made of padded cotton. Over this went a *hauberk* of chain-mail, also with long sleeves and a *coif* attached. Then plates of body armour were buckled on his breast and back, thighs and knees, and elbows and shoulders. Next he put on a long sleeveless gown, made of white linen, belted at the waist, reaching to his calves and slit up the back and front for riding. This was possibly to protect the armour from rusting in the rain. Last of all he put on mail gauntlets and his heavy *helm*. This might be flat-topped or cone-shaped and covered the whole of his face and head. There were slits to see through and little holes for ventilation. The knight's horse was well protected too, covered with leather, linen quilting or sometimes chain-mail.

Knights fought with many weapons. All carried a sword in a scabbard that hung on the left hip from a broad leather belt. Many wore also at their right side a short dagger. Other weapons used in battle were long spears, *maces* and axes. To fend off the blows from enemy weapons a knight carried also a shield, described by a modern writer as 'shaped like the bottom of an electric iron'.

It was very difficult for knights to recognise one another in battle when they wore their helms. That is why they carried a banner or small pennant attached to their spears, with a device painted on it by which they were known. This badge came to belong to a knight's family and none but they were supposed to wear it. The same design was painted on the knight's shield and linen surcoat.

A knight's followers in battle fought on foot. They were equipped with daggers, long spears or axes and sometimes slings, as well as small round shields called bucklers. Their armour was similar to a knight's, made of chain-mail or leather padding, except that they did not wear leg armour.

William Wallace

Edward Bruce

Robert Bruce

Sir James Douglas

27

Their helmets did not cover their face, but were either round caps or broad-brimmed rather like those of modern British soldiers.

LEISURE-TIME

When knights were not fighting or helping to rule the country, and ladies were not giving orders to servants, noble people had plenty of leisure. Indoors they played at chess and draughts and different games with dice. Ladies spent hours and hours at embroidery. There were few books for light reading and they were very expensive. Not every noble person could read, because, like humble people, they had little need to do so. Instead they told one another stories, sometimes very long ones, and listened eagerly while travelling minstrels told theirs in song, sometimes to their own accompaniment on the

Above: *these chessmen were found in the Hebrides and were carved out of walrus ivory*

Playing at backgammon, a game with counters and dice

38

harp. One such minstrel was Thomas the Rhymer, sometimes known as Thomas of Ercildoune, a half-legendary
person who lived at this time around Earlston in the Borders,
and whose ballads were long remembered and retold.

Jugglers and musicians too came to the castle. There was
often dancing, which must have been rather like our children's
games and folk dances, all holding hands and going round in
a circle. Children played at games that are still played, such
as ninepins and blind man's buff. They had whipping-tops
and dolls and little model animals. Young and old kept pets:
from ladies' tiny lap-dogs to monkeys for boys and girls.

Everybody spent a great deal of time in the open air.
Knights were soldiers after all, and had to keep in training.
They had mock battles called tournaments, with real weapons

Musicians. Find out what instruments they
are playing

Hawking

Jousting was obviously a dangerous sport!

and armour. No wonder that many were killed or wounded. Hunting on horseback for deer and wild boar was a favourite pastime, so was hawking, with falcons trained to bring down other birds.

THE FOOD THEY ATE

Fresh *venison* and game must have always been welcome at table when people in the castle were tired of fish, poultry and beef that was either very spicy or salty from the brine in which it was preserved. They ate bread and drank ale, too, like the common people, but they had cooks to make all kinds of delicacies: pies filled with herrings and eels, and sweets prepared from nuts, herbs and dried fruits. Ladies and gentlemen could afford wines from France and had fresh fruits from their own gardens and orchards.

There were two main meals a day, as for most people. Here is a description of a meal in a nobleman's household:

'First meat is prepared and *arrayed*, guests be called together, forms and stools be set in the hall, and tables, cloths and towels be ordained, *disposed* and made ready. Guests be set with the lord in the chief place of the table, and they sit not down at the table before the guests wash their hands. Children be set then in place, and servants at a table by themselves. First knives, spoons and salts be set on the table, and then bread and drink and many *divers messes*. Household servants busily help

At table. It was good manners to offer your neighbour a drink from your cup

each other to do everything *diligently* and talk merrily together. The guests are entertained with *lutes* and harps. Now wine and messes of meat are brought forth and departed. At the last come fruit and spices; and when they have eaten, cloths and trestles are borne away, and guests

Left: *An earthenware jug and* right: *three-legged ewer. Try to see these objects, along with the quern shown on page 14, the candlestick on page 16, the pot on page 27 and the chessmen on page 38 which are kept in the Museum of Antiquities in Edinburgh.*

Wagons like this one would be useful for carrying people and their belongings from one castle to another

wash and wipe their hands again. The grace is said and guests thank the lord. Then for gladness and comfort, drink is brought yet again.'

Notice that the writer takes for granted we understand things that were common at that time which need to be explained to readers nowadays. Guests did not eat off plates. They used trenchers of old bread cut in thick slices, on which were served the 'messes', or helpings of meat. Sodden with gravy these slices of bread were doled out to poor people after the meal was over. The host and the chief guests drank out of coloured glass and silver but everyone else had earthenware or wood. It was good manners to share your food with your neighbour and to sip from his cup, first wiping your mouth. All the while hunting dogs prowled about for the meat and bones thrown on the floor.

When the meal and the entertainment were over for the evening it was time for rest. The lord and his family retired to their chamber, but the others had to bed down where they could, on straw mattresses along benches and on the floor itself.

A noble family was always on the move, travelling from one castle to another. A great baron had many estates, some of them in England and even in France as well as in Scotland. He had to travel round them to eat up the rents from his tenants. When supplies ran out in one castle he would move on to another, taking with him not only clothes and weapons, but tables and benches, kitchen equipment and even window shutters. A noble household had to move for another reason: disease was liable to break out when large numbers of people were living together in so small a space and the drains became choked.

5 Ruling Scotland

All these people, in castle, burgh or toun, could live at peace only if the country was well governed. Everything depended on the King. He had to make laws and see that they were carried out, act as judge in disputes and defend his people against their enemies. The King had many people to help him, of course. When he needed advice or extra money to run the country he would summon his abbots, bishops and nobles to meet him on an appointed day at Perth, perhaps, or Edinburgh or Stirling for he had no fixed residence. They had to come in return for holding lands from him. When they met they made up what was called the King's Court. Sometimes they acted as a court of law. At other times they made new laws. This was the beginning of the Scottish Parliament, when they passed acts of parliament.

The King kept beside him all the time men he trusted most. These were his council. The chief members were his chancellor and chamberlain. The chancellor drew up legal documents which were recognised by the imprint on wax of the Great Seal that he guarded. The chamberlain was responsible for the royal household and looked after the King's accounts. He collected the royal revenue. In one year this amounted to £5,413 13s 0d of which £2,896 18s 3d were rents from the royal estates. Out of this income the chamberlain had to pay all the King's expenses, public as well as private, such as £5 a year to the royal gardener. He had also to inspect the King's burghs and preside over the meetings of the Court of the Four Burghs.

To keep law and order the King depended most on his sheriffs. There were twenty-six in all, each a powerful noble-man in charge of the country round about a King's burgh known as a shire. When the King went to war it was the sheriffs who mustered the followers of royal tenants to make

The two sides of the wax seal of King Alexander

up the army and strengthen royal castles. They collected rents from his tenants, the customs duties from the burghs and the fines imposed on offenders they tried in their courts. To make sure that the sheriffs were just, two judges, or justiciars, travelled round the country in spring and autumn. One was for the land north of the Firth of Forth, the other for land to the south. They also tried cases that were too difficult for the sheriffs, such as murder and robbery. In the south and east there was reasonable order, but north of the Highland Line the King's laws were often ignored. In the far north, the Hebrides and Galloway the people obeyed ancient laws of their own.

Fortunately for the people Scotland had strong kings. Under Alexander II and Alexander III the country prospered. There was peace for most of their reigns. Later people looked back and called this time a 'Golden Age'. With her neighbours Norway and England, there was friendship. In 1266 the Norwegians signed the Treaty of Perth and gave up the Hebrides to Scotland. A few years later their king, Erik, married Margaret, the daughter of Alexander III. There were close family ties with England too. Alexander III's wife was an English princess, and even after she died he was on friendly terms with her brother, King Edward I.

One matter, however, spoiled the friendship of the two · 45

kings. In the past Scottish kings had *paid homage* to the English king for the lands they held in England. King Edward claimed that this homage was due for the kingdom of Scotland, but as long as Alexander was alive he did not press this claim.

We do not know what Alexander III looked like. Chroniclers say that he was well built and handsome. From the records kept by his chamberlain we can tell that he was fond of hunting. He seems to have been happily married with a family. His last years, however, were sad. Within a few months of each other his son and his daughter, the Queen of Norway, died. In 1285 the nobles agreed that her daughter, Margaret, his only surviving descendant should succeed him. This shows how peaceful Scotland was when it was thought the country could be ruled by a queen who was only a baby! King Alexander married again but he had no more children. His little grand-daughter, the Maid of Norway, became ruler of Scotland when his body was found at Kinghorn in March 1286.

6 'When Alexander, Our King Was Dead'

This is the earliest known piece of Scottish verse:

> When Alexander our king was dead,
> That Scotland led in love and *le*   (law)
> Away with *sons* of ale and bread   (plenty)
> Of wine and wax, of game and glee.
> Our gold was changed into lead.
> Christ, born into Virginity,
> *Succour* Scotland and remedy   (help)
> That stood is in perplexity.

The unknown writer of these lines was expressing how people felt in Scotland after the death of their King. Instead of enjoying peace and prosperity they had to face war and poverty.

The Maid of Norway was too young to leave her father, so six Guardians were appointed to rule Scotland on her behalf. Then a powerful nobleman called Robert Bruce, Lord of Annandale, rose in rebellion and claimed that he was the rightful ruler of Scotland. The Guardians had no difficulty in putting down this uprising, but they could see that as long as Scotland was without a strong ruler, noblemen like the Lord of Annandale would always be able to threaten the peace of the kingdom.

King Edward of England could see this too. He did not want Scotland to fall into disorder, in case it led to trouble in England, so he watched carefully what was happening. In 1289 the King of Norway and he agreed that the young Queen of Scots should be sent to live in England. 'When the Kingdom of Scotland shall have been fully settled in quietness and peace,' they said, 'the King of England will send the Lady to Scotland.'

The Scottish Guardians approved of this arrangement and raised no objections when King Edward later told them of

A model of a ship of the time. Can you pick out the steersman, to give you an idea of the ship's size?

plans he had already made for the marriage of the young Queen to his son and heir, Prince Edward. They welcomed the idea, no doubt thinking that this marriage would keep the two countries at peace. They therefore urged the King of Norway to send his daughter to England straight away.

In July 1290 an agreement was drawn up at Birgham on the River Tweed. By this treaty the Scottish Queen was to marry the English Prince, though it was clearly stated that Scotland was to remain 'separate, apart and free in itself, without subjection to the English kingdom'. This shows the Guardians realised there was a danger that the larger kingdom, England, might swallow up its smaller neighbour, Scotland. So when King Edward demanded that English soldiers should be allowed to take over Scottish castles the Scottish Guardians firmly said no.

Meanwhile the English King was having fitted out a 'great ship' from Yarmouth to bring the little Queen over from Norway. No expense was spared to make her journey comfortable. Figs, raisins and gingerbread were ordered to be put on board, for after all she was only a little girl of seven. Finally her father agreed to let her go. It was September and rough seas rocked her ship as it made its way westwards from Bergen. The little Queen never saw her kingdom. On the way she took sick and died in Orkney and her body was taken back to be buried in Bergen.

Rumours of the Queen's death reached Scone where the Guardians had gathered to meet her. Fearing the worst, one of them, the Bishop of St Andrews, wrote to King Edward:

'The kingdom is disturbed and the people distracted. Sir Robert Bruce came with a great following, but what he intends to do or how to act, as yet we do not know. But the earls of Mar and Atholl are already collecting their army; and some other nobles of the land are won over to their party, and on that account there is fear of general war and a great slaughter of men unless Your Majesty apply a speedy remedy.'

Earnestly the Bishop begged the King to send troops to the Borders 'for the consolation of the Scottish people and for saving the shedding of blood'.

King Edward of England was the obvious person for the Guardians to turn to in this time of trouble. He was the friend and brother-in-law of their late King, and grand-uncle of the Maid of Norway. Besides, he was a most experienced ruler and famous for his great knowledge of the law. Here is how a writer of the time described him:

'In build he was elegant and of commanding stature, towering head and shoulders above the people; his hair, which in boyhood turned from silver to yellow, and in youth became black, beautified his old age with its snowy whiteness.'

Edward was a man of fifty-one and had been on the throne since 1272. He was Duke of Gascony (in France) and also 49

Lord of Ireland. Recently he had conquered Wales. Many Englishmen thought that he should make himself the master of the rest of the British Isles. This was the man who was now invited to intervene in the affairs of Scotland when it was without a King.

Who was to rule Scotland? King Alexander had left no other close relatives. Many nobles who were distantly related to him put forward claims to be King. Edward agreed to judge which of them had the best claim, and said that he would meet them in his great castle at Norham on the Tweed. Straight away he insisted that the Scots should accept him as their overlord. They had three weeks to make up their mind. Meanwhile the English army round about the castle of Norham got bigger every day. At the end of the three weeks the leading men of Scotland very politely but firmly stated that they could not accept Edward as overlord. Only the Scottish King could do this, they said, and they could not speak for him, because there was not one. We can only guess now what Edward replied to this. Within a few days, however, those nobles who had put forward claims to the Scottish throne the Competitors they are called – had all come round to acknowledge Edward as their overlord.

There were thirteen competitors but only four had claims that were considered seriously. You can see them on the family tree opposite. Study this tree carefully. The two with the best chance of being chosen to be king were Robert Bruce and John Balliol. Bruce said that he should be king because he was nearest in age to Earl David of Huntingdon, even although he was only the son of that man's younger daughter. Balliol's claim was based on the fact that he was descended from Earl David's eldest daughter. A court of 104 learned men set up to advise King Edward studied the claims carefully. Finally in November 1292 in the castle at Berwick King Edward declared that John Balliol was to be the King of Scots. This was because he was nearest in line of succession to the dead Queen, through being descended from an eldest child, Margaret, daughter of Earl David of Huntingdon.

All that remains today of the great castle of Norham

A family-tree of the Scottish Royal Family, showing the main claimants to the throne underlined

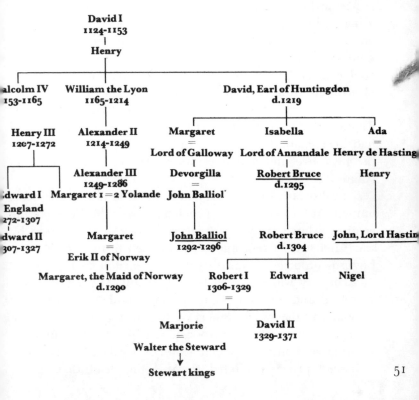

```
                        David I
                       1124-1153
                         Henry
       ┌──────────────────┼──────────────────────────────────┐
  alcolm IV      William the Lyon              David, Earl of Huntingdon
   153-1165        1165-1214                           d.1219
                                          ┌──────────────┼──────────────┐
  Henry III      Alexander II         Margaret        Isabella          Ada
  1207-1272       1214-1249               =               =               =
                                    Lord of Galloway  Lord of Annandale  Henry de Hasting
  dward I       Alexander III        Devorgilla      Robert Bruce         Henry
  England        1249-1286               =              d.1295
  272-1307   Margaret 1 = 2 Yolande  John Balliol
  dward II
  307-1327        Margaret           John Balliol    Robert Bruce     John, Lord Hastin
                     =                1292-1296         d.1304
                Erik II of Norway                  ┌──────┼──────┐
          Margaret, the Maid of Norway         Robert I   Edward   Nigel
                   d.1290                       1306-1329
                                                    =
                                          ┌─────────┴─────────┐
                                       Marjorie            David II
                                          =                1329-1371
                                   Walter the Steward
                                          ↓
                                    Stewart kings
```

51

Thus began the unhappy reign of King John. He was installed as King at Scone on 30 November (St Andrew's Day). At Christmas he paid homage to King Edward for his kingdom. Very soon he found that Edward did not intend to leave him alone to rule Scotland. Men who were dissatisfied with the justice they got in Scottish courts found King Edward ready to listen to their appeals for better treatment, although he had promised not to do this. A merchant in Gascony, for example, claimed that King John had not paid him £2,000 for supplying wine to the late King Alexander. Edward ordered King John to appear before his court at Westminster. The Scottish councillors, insulted at the way their King was being treated, prompted him not to go. But fearing that he would lose his throne if he disobeyed, King John, as a loyal vassal, answered his overlord's summons and went.

Meanwhile in 1294 Edward had gone to war with the King of France. He told the Scots to stop trading with his enemies and ordered their King to come with an army to fight them. This was the last straw. In July 1295 a council of twelve earls, barons and bishops took over the government of Scotland from King John. In his name they made a secret treaty with the French to fight on their side against the English. Agreements like this between France and Scotland had been made before and would continue to be made for the next two and a half centuries. We call this the 'Auld Alliance'.

King Edward was furious and decided to punish the Scots himself. At the end of March 1296 he crossed the Tweed at the head of a huge army and besieged Berwick by land and by sea. After a brief resistance the town fell to the English. An English chronicler describes what happened next:

'The city was occupied by the enemy. Much booty was seized and no fewer than 15,000 of both sexes perished, some by the sword, others by fire, in the space of a day and a half, and the survivors, including even little children, were sent into perpetual exile. Nevertheless, this most *clement* prince exhibited towards the dead that mercy which he had *proffered* to the living, for I myself beheld an immense number of men told off to bury the bodies of the fallen, all of whom were to receive as wages a penny apiece at the King's expense.'

Edward's fury at being thwarted had been unleashed on Scotland's richest town. Furthermore the townsfolk had jeered at him from the town walls, calling him 'Longshanks' on account of his long legs.

At Spottsmuir near Dunbar, Edward was met by an army of Scottish nobles. With his better equipped, better organised and more experienced army he put them to flight. Edinburgh Castle was bombarded with stones from siege-machines for three days until the garrison surrendered. At Stirling the garrison fled and left the porter to hand over the keys. No one seemed able to resist the invaders. The country had no leaders. Many nobles were prisoners of the English. Some were also subjects of King Edward. They were frightened to fight against him in case he took away their estates in England. As for King John, he saw that there was little point in trying to fight on and submitted to King Edward at Brechin in Angus.

To show that he was no longer fit to be king the royal emblem, the red lion of Scotland, was ripped off his tabard, or surcoat. This is probably why John Balliol was later called 'Toom Tabard', meaning 'Empty Jacket' or 'King Nobody'.

King Edward now rode in triumph through the Mearns to Aberdeen and on as far as Elgin. There he turned and went back to Berwick, passing through other main towns on the way. Wherever he went the important people of Scotland came to *swear allegiance* to him. Their names were all written down on pieces of parchment that were sewn together and known as the 'Ragman's Roll'.

Now he could rest content. Scotland had been subdued. Without a king and with the nobles divided and scattered, it seemed impossible for the Scots to rise up again. As if to make them forget that they had ever been a free people, 53

King Edward removed valuable things that might have reminded them of their freedom: these included letters and charters belonging to the government, the *regalia* from Edinburgh Castle, the holy Black *Rood* of Saint Margaret of Scotland from Holyrood Abbey, and from the Abbey of Scone the ancient Stone of Destiny. Kings of Scots had been enthroned on this stone for centuries. People believed the legend that it had been brought to Scotland by Scota, an Egyptian princess, and that it was the stone that Jacob had used as a pillow in the story told in the Bible, in Genesis, chapter 28. With these things in his possession King Edward, in his orderly way, now made arrangements for Scotland to be ruled in his name.

A piece of sandstone with an interesting history: the Coronation Stone, Scotland's Stone of Destiny

7 War of Independence: Part I

The English were everywhere, their sheriffs collecting dues and trying cases, their soldiers manning the royal castles. The Governor of Scotland was the Earl of Surrey, an elderly nobleman, who chose to remain in England because of ill-health. He left Scotland in the care of the Treasurer, Hugh Cressingham, a cruel stupid person, by all accounts, whom everybody hated because of his greed and haughty manner. He was assisted by Ormsby, the Justiciar. Some of the English officials tried to treat the Scottish people fairly, but many robbed and bullied them. No matter what they did they were hated because they were conquerors.

Thus no sooner had King Edward marched south after his conquest of Scotland than the Scots were rising against him. In the spring of 1297 Cressingham was reporting outbreaks of violence in Galloway and the West Highlands. Then came news from the north of a more serious threat to English rule in Scotland. Andrew Murray, the young son of Andrew Murray of Petty, had escaped from an English prison and made his way home to his father's castle at Avoch. There, having raised an army of farmers and townsfolk from nearby Inverness, he had stormed Castle Urquhart on Loch Ness and taken Inverness Castle itself. Scottish noblemen, sent to capture him, did nothing to stop him and may even have helped him in secret. The whole of Moray was soon overrun. Aberdeenshire and the Mearns were in danger. In Ayrshire some nobles rebelled against the English rather half-heartedly but soon surrendered to an English force at Irvine. Among them was the young Earl of Carrick, grandson of that Robert Bruce who had earlier tried unsuccessfully to be King.

In July the situation was still serious enough for Cressingham to write to King Edward for £2,000 for expenses, because, he complained: 'Not one of the sheriffs, bailiffs or officials can raise a penny of the revenues on account of a multitude of different perils which daily and continually threaten them.' Later he announced: 'In some shires the Scots have appointed and established officials. Thus no shire is properly kept, save for Berwickshire and Roxburghshire, and they only recently.'

Thus control of Scotland was quickly slipping out of English hands. The Scottish people were finding new leaders: not from the nobles, many of whom were still prisoners or allies of King Edward. Some could not make up their minds whether to risk fighting against him. Such a one was the Earl of Carrick. The leaders of the Church in Scotland resented English domination, but they had to help those who resisted in secret. Foremost among them was Robert Wishart, Bishop of Glasgow. The new leaders of Scotland were the 'middle folk', small landholders or lairds, such as Andrew Murray and, of course, William Wallace.

It was after he had murdered the sheriff of Lanark that Wallace became the open enemy of King Edward. In the same month of May 1297, he chased the Justiciar, Ormsby, from his court at Scone. A chronicler wrote: 'From that time there gathered to him all who were of a bitter heart and were weighed down beneath the burden of *bondage* under the intolerable rule of English domination. And he became their leader.'

Little definite is known about this man William Wallace. He was born about 1270, the second son of Sir William Wallace of Elderslie in Renfrewshire. On the next page you can see how a sculptor centuries later imagined how he might have looked. Blind Harry, a poet who lived about a hundred and fifty years later described him as:

> Nine quarters large he was in length – no less;
> Third part his length in shoulders broad was he,
> Right seemly, strong and handsome for to see;
> His limbs were great, with stalward pace and sound;
> His brows were hard, his arms were great and round;

– a man of great strength and very powerfully built, indeed.

This man now became King Edward's most deadly enemy. In the August of 1297 he was first reported to be in hiding in the Forest of Selkirk, later he was out in the open, besieging the castle at Dundee. Meanwhile, fresh from taking castles in Aberdeenshire and the Mearns, Andrew Murray and his men were marching south. Somewhere the two leaders joined forces. In early September at Stirling they stood together, ready to meet an English army under the Earl of Surrey, who could hardly wait to wipe out what he regarded as a band of Scottish outlaws.

The statue of William Wallace in Aberdeen, unveiled in 1888

Scots and English took up positions on either side of the River Forth: the Scots on the lower slopes of the Ochil Hills, the English at the southern end of the wooden bridge up river from Stirling. On 11 September the English began to cross the bridge. So narrow was it they had to come over in twos. On the Scots side, between the river and the hills, was a broad expanse of meadow-land or carse, over which ran a narrow causeway of firm ground.

The Scots watched below them the glittering *cavalcade* advance, with glinting spears and fluttering pennants. Behind the knights trudged the ranks of spearmen. All the English were seasoned warriors, with fighting experience gained in France and Wales, and on the Crusades. The Scots had few cavalry. They were but raw amateurs in comparison, accustomed to raids and ambushes but not to the discipline of pitched battles. Their strength lay in the skill of their foot-soldiers, lightly armoured and equipped with spears twelve-feet long and daggers. They were also fighting for their freedom.

A good number of the English had crossed the bridge and were jostling for position on the soft carse when Wallace sounded his horn and the Scots charged. Their right wing swung round and cut the English off from the bridge, while the rest charged into the body of the English army: spearmen against knights. Soon there was confusion in the English ranks. Horses reared and stumbled, their riders thrown on to the carse, while the Scottish spearmen lunged in amongst the helpless mass. Some knights frantically tried to ford the river, but in vain with their weighty armour. On the bridge itself, those retreating in disorder were trapped by others still trying to cross. Men and chargers plunged to their death in the swirling waters of the River Forth.

Soon all was over. The English were scattered or slain. The Earl of Surrey fled and, it was said, reined his horse only when he reached Berwick. Booty and ransom waited on the field of battle to be collected from the fallen knights. From among the dead, the body of the hated Cressingham was picked out.

In savage revenge the victors flayed it and cut it up in strips as mementoes of the Battle of Stirling Bridge.

It is hard to imagine the effect this defeat had on the English. In their eyes, till now, the Scots had appeared to be poor fighters who were easily put to flight. But now, until they got another army together, they had to watch in dismay as one by one castles fell to the Scots, until only four were left in English hands. Even Berwick was recaptured. In October and November the war was carried into England. Farms and villages in the northern counties were burned down and the cattle and grain were taken away. Carlisle was besieged. Everywhere the cry of horror was heard, 'The Scots are coming!' An English chronicler wrote bitterly, 'In that time the praise of God ceased in all the monasteries and churches from Newcastle to Carlisle. For all the monks and priests with almost the whole population had fled from the face of the Scots.'

Murray and Wallace were now the real rulers of Scotland. Amid the fighting they found time to plan for the future and encourage trade. Here is part of a letter they wrote at Haddington. The merchants of Hamburg and Lübeck in Germany, '. . . may have a safe access to all parts of the kingdom of Scotland with their merchandise because the kingdom of Scotland, thanks to God, is recovered from the power of the English.'

Many of the Scottish nobles were now encouraged to join the war against the English, though some were reluctant to fight under leaders who were not great barons. Then in November Andrew Murray died, possibly from wounds received at Stirling Bridge. This was a great loss. Wallace, however, carried on the war. In March 1298 he was appointed Guardian of Scotland and thereafter known as 'Sir' William Wallace.

All this time King Edward had been out of England fighting the French. Now he returned, determined to deal with the Scots once again in person. He moved his government departments from London to York, which shows that he 59 expected the campaign to last long, and assembled the greatest army ever seen in the north of England: 2,000 knights and 12,000 footsoldiers, including a large force of crossbowmen and archers from Wales. Burning and laying waste as they went, this army marched up Lauderdale towards the coast, the Scots retreating before them. Ships with food-supplies followed the army off shore towards Leith.

To the east of Falkirk the Scots halted and on 22 July faced the English. Once again the Scots were weaker in numbers and had few cavalry and only a handful of archers from Selkirk Forest. But they were in good spirits from recent successes. Besides, the English were in poor shape after their long forced march. There was not enough food for the army and many men were sick. The supply ships had not kept up with the army. Some soldiers had mutinied. King Edward was in great pain from a kick in his side from his horse.

As at Stirling Wallace's men had taken up a good defensive position. With rough wooded country behind them, they were drawn up on a hillside with a small loch in front. An Englishman who was present described the battle.

'They [the Scots] had drawn up all their men in four circular bodies called *schiltrons,* composed of spearmen, with their spears pointing upwards; they were joined one to another and stood with their faces turned towards the circumference of the circles. Between the circles were spaces occupied by archers; in the extreme rear were the cavalry.'

These schiltrons, composed of possibly a thousand men each, must have looked a formidable sight. So also to a spearman was a mass of mounted knights. It was like modern infantry drawn up against tanks. But the English had a more deadly weapon still, as the Battle of Falkirk showed.

The English cavalry advanced, then split in two, each division making its way round the loch to attack the flanks of the Scottish army. The battle was hard and long. According to the English account:

60 'As soon as our men approached the Scots cavalry fled

without striking a blow, a few only remaining to give orders to the footsoldiers.'

With no knights to protect them the Scottish bowmen were mown down by the English knights. Then:

'Our men proceeded to attack the Scots spearmen. While our horsemen could not advance for the number of spears, those of the enemy on the outside struck out and pierced several with their spears. But our footsoldiers shot at them with arrows, and securing a quantity of round stones, of which there was plenty near, stoned them. So when many had been slain, and others confounded, the remainder of the outer ring were thrown back on the others, and our horsemen broke in and swept the field.'

It was the archers who won the day. With their longbows over five feet in length firing arrows of over three feet, they would help to win many a battle for England in the future.

The English did not follow up their victory but retreated hurriedly. Supplies were short and King Edward was needed in France, where he was to remain for most of the next six years. After Falkirk the Scots dared not risk another pitched battle. Instead they waged what we would call guerrilla warfare, attacking and ambushing in small numbers, though there was one battle with a light English force at Roslin in 1303. Yet far from being downhearted the Scots were even more determined to go on fighting and the English were confined to Galloway and the burghs of the south-east.

Wallace resigned as Guardian after his defeat at Falkirk. As a Scottish writer put it, he 'chose rather to serve with the

English archers at practice

crowd than to be set over them to their ruin and the greivous wasting of the people'. For the next seven years we lose track of his movements. His place as Guardian was taken by others: first by Robert Bruce, Earl of Carrick and John Comyn, Lord of Badenoch. They often disagreed, however. Comyn was a relative of the exiled King John, the rival of Bruce's grandfather. On at least one occasion Bruce and Comyn came to blows in public. With such divided leadership the Scots had little chance of winning back their freedom.

During these seven years Wallace was abroad looking for help. For a time the Pope and the King of France gave him support until it suited them both to make peace with England in 1303. This left King Edward free to leave France and march an army into Scotland. Stirling Castle was in Scottish hands, blocking his route to the north. Three floating bridges were therefore towed up from King's Lynn in Norfolk and placed across the River Forth to carry his army over to Fife, thus by-passing Stirling. He marched as far north as Kinloss Abbey in Moray and returned to spend the winter at Dunfermline Abbey, which he ordered to be burnt down when he left.

During this time most of the Scottish nobles gave in to him again. He forgave them for fighting against him and spared them their lands. To the defenders of Stirling he was not so merciful. For three months they had held out, despite famine against thirteen *siege-engines*, including Edward's 'war-wolf', the latest model which was said to hurl stones of over two hundredweight.

To Wallace and any others who refused to surrender Edward was pitiless. He instructed that 'No words of peace are to be held out to William Wallace in any circumstance whatsoever unless he places himself utterly and absolutely in our will.'

Wallace was finally taken near Glasgow on 3 August 1305. He was handed over to the English by Sir John Menteith, a loyal supporter of King Edward. He was taken for trial to London and lodged in the home of a leading citizen in

How a nineteenth century artist showed a siege.
Note the different kinds
of siege—craft

Fenchurch Street. On Monday 23rd he was led in procession to Westminster Hall with the Mayor of London and the other judges chosen to try him. The charges were read out that he had murdered the sheriff of Lanark and committed many other crimes including treason. To all these he pleaded guilty except treason, because, he said, he had never accepted the King of England as his overlord nor promised to serve him. The judges found him guilty. The penalty was death.

Wallace could expect no mercy. The English loathed him. They took him and tied him to a *hurdle* and he was dragged by a horse through the dusty streets to Smithfield. A jeering crowd watched him hang. While still alive, he was taken down, savagely disembowelled, then beheaded and quartered. His head was stuck on a pole and displayed on London Bridge; the four parts of his body were put up as a warning to those who resisted King Edward in Newcastle, Berwick, Stirling and Perth.

Now King Edward thought he could rest content. Scotland was at peace and might now be governed as a part of England. Scots and English, he hoped, would learn to live as friends again under the same King. King Edward's hopes for the future, however, were rudely shattered with news that reached him in the following February of a murder committed in a church at Dumfries.

8 War of Independence : Part II

King Edward could scarcely believe the news that messengers brought him. Two leading Scottish noblemen, Robert Bruce, Earl of Carrick and John Comyn, Lord of Badenoch, had quarrelled in the Church of the Greyfriars in Dumfries and Bruce had slain Comyn. So powerful and well-connected were these men that this murder, the more so since it had been committed in a church, was bound to shatter the peace of Scotland. The murderer would have to be punished.

Exactly what happened in the church at Dumfries on that February night in 1306 no one knows. The two men had arranged to meet to discuss how to free Scotland. They knew that John Balliol did not want to return from exile in France, and yet they were sure that most Scotsmen wanted a king. Both of them had strong claims to the throne. Comyn was Balliol's nephew and he had experience of ruling Scotland as one of the Guardians. Bruce, too, had been a Guardian and he was head of one of Scotland's most noble families. According to one story, Comyn and he made a pact that each should help the other to become King. The one that failed would receive the other's estates. Bruce, it is said, accused Comyn of betraying this plan to King Edward, thus forcing him to flee for his life. Comyn and Bruce had quarrelled before when they were joint Guardians. Now, it seemed, Bruce struck Comyn. A scuffle followed among their men and Comyn was killed. It was an accident almost certainly, as Bruce would not deliberately plan to commit murder in a church.

Though people did not know it at the time, this was the second round of the Scottish War of Independence. The man who was to lead the Scots was then aged thirty-two, the holder of many manors in England as well as vast estates in Ayrshire, Galloway and Aberdeenshire. Robert Bruce had fought on

This map shows places mentioned in the book that are connected with the War of Independence

Orkney

50 Miles

H E B R I D E S

Kinloss
Avoch
LAIGH
OF MORAY
Elgin
Castle
Urquhart
Inverurie
BADENOCH
Kildrummy
THE MOUNTH
MEARNS
Pass of Brander
BREADALBANE
Scone
Arbroath
Dalry (Tyndrum)
Methven
Dundee
L. Lomond
R. Forth
Ochil Hills
St. Andrews
Stirling
Kinghorn
Bannockburn
The Ferry
Dirleton
Glasgow
Falkirk
Leith
Dunbar
Edinburgh
Haddington
Elderslie
Roslin
LAUDERDALE
Loudoun Hill
Earlston
Berwick
Arran
Irvine
Birgham
Norham
Dunaverty
Prestwick
ANNANDALE
Rathlin
Turnberry
Glentrool
Annan
Dumfries
Lanercost
Carlisle
Burgh
on Sands
Solway Firth
Firth of Clyde

I R E L A N D

the side of Wallace in his struggle for Scottish independence, though latterly he had made peace with King Edward. This was possibly because he saw it was pointless to fight for John Balliol, a member of a rival family and a man who showed that he was no leader of men. King Edward had forgiven Bruce and showed that he thought highly of him. Yet Bruce had probably always intended to claim the Scottish throne. Only with a King at their head would the Scots ever rally against the English. With the murder of Comyn, Bruce now seized the chance of putting himself at their head. There was no turning back for him.

An Englishman tells us what happened next in a letter he wrote from Berwick:

'Sir, the news in these parts is this, that the Earl of Carrick holds the King's castles of Dumfries and Ayr and the castle of Dalswinton that belonged to John Comyn. He has his castle of Loch Doon in Carrick and the castle of Dunaverty in Kintyre *victualled* for a long period. [He] has made war in Galloway to cause the people to rebel with him, but they have answered *in accord* that they will never rebel against the King for any man living.'

Other strongholds fell to Bruce and with the help of the Bishop of Glasgow he was 'attempting to seize the realm of Scotland'.

At the end of March Bruce went to Scone Abbey where in the past Scottish Kings had been crowned and installed on the ancient Stone of Destiny. The English had taken it away, however, along with the crown of Scotland.

Bruce was made King without either crown or Stone of Destiny. Only a few nobles and leading clergymen were present at the simple ceremony. The Bishop of Glasgow even loaned the King robes for the occasion. The young Earl of Fife, who should have led the King to his throne, was absent. His sister, the Countess of Buchan, braved danger, however, to come and perform this act on his behalf and also placed a simple gold coronet on Bruce's head. So began the reign of Robert the First, King of Scots.

The King of England, meanwhile, was determined to tame the Scots and their so-called King once for all. Solemnly he swore vengeance on the murderer Bruce. Despite a creeping illness, probably cancer, that weakened him daily, he prepared for yet another campaign in Scotland that he intended to lead in person. His cousin, the Earl of Pembroke, was given charge of Scottish affairs with full power to hunt down Bruce and his supporters. This is what was to happen to one of them: 'We command you [Pembroke] to burn down all his manors, to destroy his lands and goods and to strip his gardens clean so that nothing is left, for an example to others like him.'

In the middle of June the Earl of Pembroke's men scattered King Robert's small army in their first battle, at Methven, north-west of Perth. For the next six months Bruce was King only in name. 'King Hob', the English called him. He was always on the run with his wife and family and their few followers. This is how John Barbour, later in the century, described these hard times in his famous epic poem, 'The Bruce':

> As outlaws went they many a day
> Among the hills, and fed on meat
> And water, nor had else to eat . . .
> Thus in the mountains *sojourned* he
> Till most men in his company
> Were ragged and torn. They had, besides,
> No shoes but those they made of hides.

They were now in the hills of Breadalbane, with enemies all around: as well as the English there were the relatives of the murdered Comyn. In an attempt to break out westwards Bruce was beaten in a *skirmish* at Dalry near Tyndrum in Strathfillan. Winter was now approaching and so he decided to send his young brother Nigel with Elizabeth, his Queen, and Marjorie, his daughter, aged twelve, along with their ladies to the castle of Kildrummy. He then struck out to the south-west to get help from the men of Lennox. On the way

The statue of King Robert at Bannockburn

In the hills of Breadalbane

they had to cross Loch Lomond. The boat was so small that they had to cross only three at a time, while some swam over. They got some food from the Earl of Lennox, then made for Bruce's castle of Dunaverty in Kintyre. But the English were hot on their heels and were soon besieging the castle, too late, however, to catch Bruce and his men who had fled across the sea to Rathlin off the coast of Ireland.

From September 1306 until the following February King Robert was in hiding. Rathlin, however, is a small island, only five miles long and one mile wide, and there was little point in his staying there when he could be seeking help elsewhere. Some historians say he went to Norway, others that he got help from friends in Ireland and among the southern islands of the Hebrides. No one knows for sure.

It was possibly during these months when he was a hunted man that word reached him of what had happened to his family and friends. The news must have made him very sad. King Edward had *confiscated* his estates and given them to Bruce's enemies. King Robert's wife and daughter had been forced to flee from Kildrummy before the English burned it down, but they had been captured and were now in separate English prisons. Nigel Bruce had been brutally executed and so had the King's friends. His sister and the Countess of Buchan, who had attended his coronation, also suffered: each was put in a cage that was specially built to King Edward's instructions, and shut away in a castle. The Bishop of St Andrews and the Bishop of Glasgow were in prison too. All King Robert's supporters were excommunicated by the Pope, a terrible punishment, because it meant that they were cut off from the Church. The task of freeing Scotland must have seemed hopeless. In the centuries afterwards a legend grew up that Bruce took heart again from watching the determined efforts of a spider to spin its web. If a spider could try, try and succeed, so then could he. In the following spring he decided to return to Scotland.

First of all he had to be sure that the people on the mainland would rise and follow him. First they crossed to the island of Arran; about fifteen miles away were his estates in Carrick and his castle of Turnberry. He sent over a scout to find out if his tenants were still loyal to him. If they were, he would signal by lighting a fire on a hill on a certain day. Keenly the King watched the shore-line opposite. At long last he spied a coil of smoke, then the flames of a fire. Eagerly, as darkness was falling he and his men rowed over. There on the beach stood the scout. But there had been a dreadful mistake. The fire had not been lit by him.

In fact he had come to warn the King that his tenants were not willing to fight for him, the English had so strong a grip on the land. Quickly the King made up his mind: he would stay and show himself to his people and lead them against the enemy.

He took to the hills of the south-west, attacking the English here and there, relying on speed and daring but rarely risking pitched battles. In April he trapped some English in Glentrool, in May he defeated others at Loudon Hill. These were small victories, but slowly he attracted more and more support.

A Scottish Lord on the English side wrote:

'I fully believe that if he can get away beyond the *Mounth* he will find the people all ready at his will more entirely than ever unless King Edward can send more troops, for there are many people living loyally in his peace so long as the English are in power. May it please God to prolong King Edward's life, for men say openly that when he is gone the victory will go to Bruce.'

But King Edward's life was not spared. He died on 7 July 1307 at Burgh-on-Sands overlooking the Solway Firth. His son, who now became king as Edward II, had promised to carry on fighting, but he chose instead to retreat southwards. He laid his father's body to rest in Westminster Abbey. This is what was later inscribed on his tomb in Latin:

HIC IACET EDWARDUS PRIMUS, MALLEUS SCOTTORUM

PACTUM SERVA

(in English, HERE LIES EDWARD FIRST,

THE HAMMER OF THE SCOTS KEEP TROTH)

The tomb of Edward I in Westminster Abbey

Unlike his father, Edward II was not interested in fighting. He was twenty-three years of age and well-built. He preferred to spend his time looking after his estates. Hunting and swimming were his favourite pastimes, and he was very fond of music and play-acting. Many of his nobles thought that these were not the sort of things a King ought to be interested in. Soon Edward began to quarrel bitterly with his nobles, and so he had little time to attend to Scotland. The death of Edward I was therefore a blessing to the Scots.

During the next seven years King Robert gradually won control of Scotland. His enemies in Galloway were crushed, and the Comyns were routed in battle, first at Inverurie in Aberdeenshire and then at the Pass of Brander in Argyll. Their lands and livestock in the north-east were destroyed.

This savage destruction was called the 'herschip' of Buchan. Says the 'Lanercost Chronicle':

> In all this fighting the Scots were so divided that often a father was with the Scots and his son with the English. Or one brother was with the Scots and another with the English, or even one individual was first on one side and then on the other. But all or most of those Scots who were with the English were with them insincerely or to save their lands in England, for their hearts if not their bodies were always with their own people.

More and more nobles were joining his side. In a parliament that met at St Andrews in 1309 they openly acknowledged him as King. The leaders of the Church, too, were behind him, despite the Pope's hostility to a man who had committed murder in a church.

Though it is true that King Robert was successful because the English were too busy at home with troubles of their own to bother with him, much of his success was due to his own efforts. He was an inspiration to his people. When all seemed hopeless he fought on. When they were leaderless, he stepped forward. Many a time he risked his life. When he was attacking the castle at Perth he led his men across the icy waters of the moat and was among the first to climb over the wall. He was a skilful general. In pitched battle and on guerilla raids he showed a keen sense of knowing where to place his men so that they would be most useful. His followers were devoted to him. Chief among them were his nephew, Thomas Randolph, Earl of Moray, and his great friend, Sir James Douglas.

In 1311 and 1312 the Scots were once again ravaging the northern counties of England. In vain the local people called for help from their King. Instead, they had to pay the Scots to go away. They probably paid out about £20,000. With this money King Robert bought supplies, corn from Ireland and weapons and armour from Germany and the Low Countries.

The English still clung to the Scottish castles. Since the Scots did not have siege engines to knock down the walls, they had to take the castles by surprise. One by one they were recaptured.

This is how Linlithgow Castle fell. One morning the English soldiers allowed in as usual the farmer Binnie with his cart full of hay. Suddenly the driver cut the traces of the oxen and the cart was stuck in the open gateway, thus preventing the soldiers from closing the gate. Binnie then shouted and out leapt from under the hay eight armed Scotsmen. They overpowered the guards and were quickly joined by other men who had been lying in wait outside. The castle was soon theirs.

Roxburgh Castle was better defended than Linlithgow but it was Fastern's Eve (Shrove Tuesday) and the garrison were off-guard, celebrating before Lent. Stealthily Sir James Douglas and his men crept up to the walls in single file, their armour hidden in the darkness by cloaks. Two men on lookout in the castle mistook them for cattle. With the help of scaling ladders made by a local man called Sim, Sir James's men climbed the wall. Suddenly a watchman was roused by the scrape of metal hooks on the stone battlements. If Sim had not quickly silenced him the alarm would have been sounded. The garrison were surprised and there was a fierce struggle until the warden of the castle surrendered.

Sir Thomas Randolph found Edinburgh Castle impossible to take because it stood on so steep a rock. Then a man called Francis said that he knew a way up the rock. As a young man, when he had been stationed at the castle, he had often visited his girl-friend in town after the gates were closed at night by using a secret path down the rock and returning the same way unseen. Once again Francis climbed the same path one night, followed by Randolph and about thirty of his most daring men. Silently they pulled themselves up the cold, bare slabs and slithery crevices, clinging by their fingers and toes to the narrow footholds. One slip would mean death and discovery and the certain failure of the whole plan. For a while they rested on a narrow shelf of rock. Suddenly they heard the voices of the guards above them. 'I see you!' one of them called out, and a stone hurtled down below. Randolph's men

An eighteenth century engraving of Edinburgh Castle Rock

hardly dared to breathe. Then the guards laughed and moved on talking loudly. It had been only a joke! Up the raiders clambered, threw their ladder on to the wall and climbed into the castle. Once again there was a struggle, the gates were opened and in rushed the main forces of besiegers. Like the other castles Edinburgh was pulled down, just in case it was retaken by the English.

By the summer of 1313 Stirling was the last important castle still in English hands. Edward Bruce, the King's brother, had besieged it for months, but the garrison was able to hold out with supplies brought from Berwick by sea. Neither side, however, could hold out for ever. Finally Edward Bruce made an agreement with the castle governor, Sir Philip Moubray, that unless an army came within three *leagues* to relieve the castle by midsummer 1314, the English would surrender it. Here was a challenge for both sides. Would the English be able to settle their own differences and come up with an army? Stirling was their last stronghold in Scotland: once they had lost Stirling Scotland was as good as lost too. If the English brought an army King Robert would finally be forced to fight in the open in a pitched battle, the kind of battle the English had a better chance of winning with their greater numbers than the Scots. Much would depend on whether the English came.

75

9 The Battle of Bannockburn, 23–24 June 1314

Bringing up military supplies

King Edward and his barons stopped quarrelling in order to save Stirling. By Christmas 1313 he had ordered them to join him with their knights at Berwick on 10 June, ready 'to put down and suppress the wicked rebellion of Robert Bruce and his accomplices in the King's land of Scotland'. An army of about 2,000 knights and some 15,000 footsoldiers from all parts of England and Wales duly assembled. Among those present were some of King Robert's Scottish enemies, including the son of the murdered John Comyn. There were also a few French and Dutch knights who came along for the love of fighting. 'Never in our time,' said an English writer 'did such an army quit England.' To keep it supplied with food, a fleet of ships from almost every port in England sailed off-shore, accompanying the army northwards.

King Robert's army was nothing like so large: probably no more than about 5,000 all of them spearmen and archers, except for some 500 lightly mounted knights. What the Scots lacked in weight and numbers, however, they made up for in courage. For seven years they had been fighting successfully together under a leader they loved and respected. At the end of May they began to gather to the south of Stirling in the Torwood.

In these positions the Scots were safe from attack on all sides, as you will see if you look at the map on p. 78. The English would approach from the south, and would have to cross the Bannockburn in its narrow *defile*. The English in Stirling were unlikely to attack because of the agreement their commander, Sir Philip Moubray, had made with Edward Bruce. If he attacked he would be breaking the rules of war, as it was fought at that time, and he would have been considered as a 'false knight'. The Scots were able to look out to the east, towards the River Forth, over the broad flat carse of Stirling, then known as the Polles or the Pows. Though parts of it were dry in summer it was covered by peat-bogs and many streams, of which the Bannockburn was by far the biggest. This stream ran through an area of drier cultivated ground that climbed gently westwards up from the carse for about half a mile. Across the Bannockburn ran the old road from the south and on through the New Park towards Stirling. The English would come along this road, and so on each side of it the Scots dug small pits and covered them with sticks and grass. Thus the English Knights would have to bunch close together and advance in small numbers.

On Saturday, 22 June, Scottish scouts sighted the English army approaching from Falkirk, amid clouds of dust thrown up by the pounding horse-beats. Since crossing the Tweed five days earlier the men had hardly rested. Following his father's route up Lauderdale to Edinburgh, Edward II had paused only to allow stragglers to catch up and to bring supplies ashore through the port of Leith. Then they were on their way westwards, marching twenty miles in a day. King Robert's scouts reported that despite the heat from marching in armour in midsummer, the English were in good shape. 77

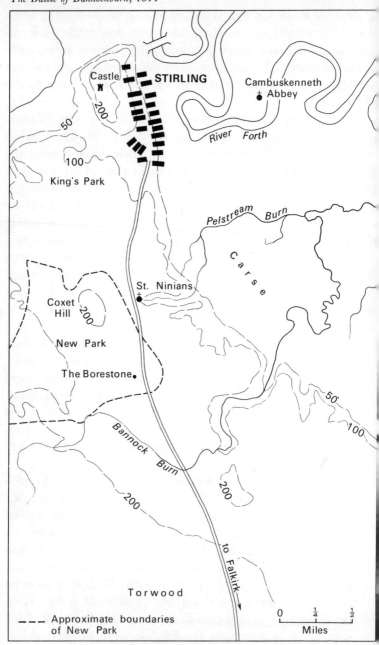

Castle

STIRLING

Cambuskenneth
+ Abbey

200

50

River Forth

100

King's Park

Pelstream Burn

C a r s e

Coxet
Hill

200

St. Ninians
+

New Park

The Borestone

50

100

Bannock Burn

200

200

to Falkirk

Torwood

— — — Approximate boundaries
of New Park

0   ¼   ½

Miles

King Robert very wisely kept this news from his own men.

By this time the Scottish King had moved his men into positions in the New Park nearer Stirling. They were arranged in four 'battles' or divisions: the *van* under Randolph, two others under Edward Bruce and Sir James Douglas, while he himself commanded the rear. In a valley to the west out of sight were left the 'sma' folk', farmers, youngsters and other non-combatants in charge of supplies.

Next day, the van of the English army entered the Torwood. Led by the Earl of Gloucester, Constable of England, and the Earl of Hereford, the van was made up of the most dashing and eager young knights of the army. Seeing the Scots who seemed to be in retreat, they spurred their horses. For what happened next let Barbour tell us:

> And when King Robert saw them there
> In battle order coming near,
> He set his own men in array.
> He rode upon a small *palfrey*,
> Handsome and light; and axe in hand,
> He set his army as he planned.
> And high upon his *basinet*,
> A leather hat and crown were set,
> So that it might be evident
> That he was king where'er he went.
> When Hereford and Gloucester were,
> With their division, coming near,
> In front of all came one that rode
> With spear in hand and *target* broad.
> Sir Henry de Bohun his name,
> A valiant knight of worthy fame,
> And cousin to Lord Hereford.
> In armour fine and bright he rode,
> Spurring his steed a bowshot clear
> In front of all the others there.
> He recognised the King, that then
> Was settling in array his men,
> And by the crown that, as I said,

Was mounted high above his head.
Toward the King forthwith rode he.
The King beheld him openly
Riding in front of all his force,
And straight at him he steered his horse.
And when Sir Henry saw him there
Come forth without a sign of fear,
Against him at full speed rode he.
He thought that he would easily
Unseat and have him at his will,
Seeing that he was horsed so ill.
Together charged they galloping.
Sir Henry missed the noble King!
And he, that in his stirrups stood,
Lifted his axe, so sharp and good,
And such a mighty stroke he aimed
That neither hat nor helmet stemmed
The force of that tremendous blow.
Down did the bold Sir Henry go.
The hand-axe shaft was broke in two.
His skull was almost cleft right through,
And there he lay, *bereft of* might.
So fell the first stroke of the fight.

How a nineteenth cent
artist imagined the fig
between Bruce and de
Bohun

This engagement was only part of a short skirmish between some of the English van and the Scottish rearguard. Edward Bruce's division joined in and the English were forced back.

Another incident which raised Scottish morale and shook English confidence took place around the same time not far away. About 300 English knights under Sir Robert Clifford set off over the carse to try to ride round the Scots' left flank in order to reach Stirling. Randolph, who ought to have seen this move and stopped it, was quickly sent by the King to catch them. Near St. Ninian's Kirk the Scottish spearmen formed a schiltron, bristling like a giant hedgehog. The English turned, unable to resist this chance to wipe out some of the enemy. They formed up and charged but found that they could not break the Scottish ranks. Many were knocked off their horses and were soon at the mercy of the Scottish spearmen. Some were captured, others fled to Stirling or back to their own lines. The way to Stirling was blocked and twice in one day Scottish infantry had thrown back English cavalry.

In the meantime, King Edward had moved up with the rest of the English army. About now Sir Philip Moubray came from the Castle, presumably under a flag of truce, to to tell him not to come any closer, as the Scots could block the way to Stirling—something the vanguard had already found out for themselves!

Men and horses, however, needed food and rest, so during the Sunday evening the English army began to cross the Bannockburn on open ground down on the carse and rested.

In the half-light of midsummer's eve there was little sleep for the English soldiers. They were also rather depressed because of two defeats in the one day and the chance that the Scots might attack before dawn. If only the English had known that the Scottish leaders were then planning to retreat to the west. Then came to King Robert, Alexander Seton, a Scotsman who had been on the English side. He told the Scots what the English were like. To the delight of his men King Robert decided to stay and fight.

During the night the English cavalry seem to have moved up on to the firmer ground of the carse, between the Bannockburn and the Pelstream. King Robert saw that his enemies were now in a very narrow space and realised that this was his chance. Before ordering his men to advance he addressed them. Centuries later, Robert Burns in his patriotic song, 'Bruce's Address to his Troops at Bannockburn' imagined the King beginning in this way:

'Scots, wha hae wi' Wallace bled,
Scots, wham Bruce has often led,
Welcome to your gory bed,
    Or to victorie.
Now's the day, and now's the hour;
See the front o' battle lour!
See approach proud Edward's power—
    Chains and slaverie!'

The Scots advanced at dawn. They were in their four divisions, led by Edward Bruce on the right, followed in turn by Randolph and Douglas, with the King bringing up the rear. The English could hardly believe what they saw: the Scots in force, risking a battle in the open—mere spearmen against an army of horsemen! Hurriedly they made ready.

The fighting began with each side firing a *salvo* of arrows, the English scoring heavily with their superior longbows. Then, as Edward Bruce's men advanced, the English vanguard charged. The Scots formed a schiltron and threw them back. Under the strain of the Scots resistance the English fell apart and their commander, the Earl of Gloucester, was killed. Now Randolph and Douglas moved up with their divisions against the rest of the English army. But so pressed together were the English between the Bannockburn and the Pelstream that they got in one another's way. Relentlessly the Scottish schiltrons reformed and pressed forward. Helplessly the English cavalry stumbled and floundered. Then, desperately, some of the English archers managed to pull themselves out from the struggling mass of knights.

King Robert had foreseen this danger, however, and he sent

Sir Robert Keith with his 500 light cavalry to charge them. With the English archers knocked out of the battle, victory for the Scots was almost assured. Now King Robert unleashed his own men who had been patiently waiting. They came from Carrick and the Isles, and with shouts (no doubt in Gaelic) of 'On them, on them, they fail!' they plunged into battle. The English were thrown back in even greater confusion among the streams and pools of the carse. Then worse followed. A fresh army seemed to be streaming out of the Torwood to the help of the Scots, with banners waving. This was the 'sma' folk', who had been kept away from the battle but who now were joining in the fighting, with make-shift banners of poles and sheets and brandishing spears. This was too much. King Edward, who had fought gallantly alongside his men, was finally persuaded to flee for safety. Off he went with his body-guard, Douglas in hot pursuit. There was no refuge for the English King at Stirling, so he turned and rode as fast as he could to Dunbar, where he took a boat for Berwick.

The battle was over. English soldiers were fleeing in all directions, some towards Stirling, others in the direction of the River Forth. A few flung themselves blindly into the thick of the fighting! Many were suffocated in their armour.

Bannockburn was a colossal defeat for the English. Many English and Welsh soldiers were murdered as they tried to trudge back home. Noblemen were more fortunate: they were taken prisoner and held for ransom. Some in fact were very chivalrously sent home without any ransom being demanded. The Earl of Hereford was released in exchange for King Robert's wife and daughter, his sister and the Bishop of Glasgow. Over £200,000 of valuable equipment (equivalent to millions of pounds in today's money) was captured.

Meanwhile Stirling Castle was handed over and Sir Philip Moubray entered King Robert's service.

For the Scots Bannockburn was more than a battle won in a long, hard war. They did not know it at the time, but it made them a free people again, ruled by a man who had proved to them and the world that he was fit to be their King.

10 After Bannockburn

Although the English had been beaten at Bannockburn it was a long time before they would admit that Robert Bruce was the rightful King of a free Scotland. What is more, they persuaded the Pope not to accept him either. The war, therefore, went on. Now, however, it was the people of northern England who had to bear the brunt of the fighting. Year after year Scottish armies, riding on little ponies called 'hobins', burned and raided as far south as Yorkshire. King Edward did little to stop them. When he did come north; he and his Queen were more than once nearly captured. At Myton in Yorkshire and later at Old Byland, English armies were put to flight in battle. There was fighting in Ireland, too. There Edward Bruce made himself King and led the Irish against the English. In 1323 Scots and English finally agreed to a truce to last for thirteen years but it was soon broken.

The Scottish people loyally supported their King in this struggle to persuade the English to recognise him as an independent ruler and so end the war. The nobles showed their determination to fight for Scotland's freedom in a letter they sent to the Pope. It was drawn up and sealed at Arbroath in 1320, probably by Bernard Linton, Abbot of Arbroath, and King Robert's chancellor. After explaining how they had come to be fighting the English they declared: 'For so long as one hundred men shall remain alive we shall never under any circumstances submit to the domination of the English. For it is not for glory or riches or honours that we fight but for freedom alone, which no good man will give up except with his life.' Even if King Robert should give up fighting for Scotland's independence, they said, they would carry on the struggle under a new king. This famous letter is known as the Declaration of Arbroath, and it is one of the earliest and most defiant declarations of independence in the world.

At last, in 1328 the English gave in and recognised that Scotland was an independent country. In the previous year King Edward II had been put off the throne and brutally murdered. The new government in England under his young son, Edward III, agreed to a treaty that was signed at Edinburgh and Northampton. The Scots were to pay £20,000 in instalments, and to try to ensure peace between the two countries a marriage was arranged. Later in the same year, at Berwick, amid great rejoicing, the wedding took place of Edward III's sister, Joan, to King Robert's young son, David. About the same time the English agreed to return the Stone of Destiny, but the citizens of London refused to let it go.

After such a long war there were many problems for King Robert to tackle. Money was very short, and so the burgesses from the royal burghs agreed in a Parliament held at Cambuskenneth, near Stirling, in 1326, to pay over a tenth of their revenues to help the King. In this way the royal burghs became represented in the Scottish parliament. People had to get used again to living in peace. There was also the question of those Scottish nobles who had fought on the English side against King Robert. It was decided that if they still wanted to be considered as Scots they would have to give up their estates in England and swear allegiance to the King of Scots. If they chose to keep their English estates and would not obey King Robert their lands in Scotland were confiscated. They came to be called the 'Disinherited' and they gave Scotland much trouble in years to come when they and their descendants tried hard to get their lands back. As for those who had served the King faithfully, they were all rewarded with grants of land. Randolph and Douglas became two of the greatest landholders in Scotland and continued to advise the King.

King Robert I ruled wisely. 'Good King Robert' the people called him. They knew they could turn to him for help in time of trouble. After all, he had shared their hardships in the past. Often they would find him in his new house at Cardross on the shores of the Firth of Clyde. There he loved to watch his ships sailing past, or to hunt in the woods round about, when he could get away from affairs of state. It was here that he died on 7 June 1329.

The King had not been very happy in his last years, because his closest relations died: first his wife, then his brother, Edward, in Ireland, and Marjorie, his daughter, the wife of Walter the Steward, in giving birth to a son called Robert. The years of campaigning in all weathers sapped the King's strength. All the while he was saddened by the fact that the Pope had not lifted the ban of excommunication from him. Not until a week after his death did word come to Scotland that the Pope had removed it already and recognised him as

King of Scots.

In his dying moments King Robert had turned to his friend and companion in battle, the 'Good Sir James Douglas', to perform one last duty: to take his heart when he was dead to the Holy Sepulchre at Jerusalem, since he had not been able to go there himself on a crusade. Before the King's body was buried in Dunfermline Abbey the heart was duly removed. Sir James took the heart, embalmed it and embarked with it carefully laid in a special casket. On the way to the Holy Land, however, he fell in with some crusaders who were fighting the Moors in Spain. In a battle Sir James was killed. Afterwards his body was brought back to Scotland and so, too, was the box with the King's heart, which was buried in

Where King Robert's body was buried in Dunfermline Abbey

Melrose Abbey. According to one modern writer the box was discovered by chance during excavations in the Abbey some years ago but secretly buried again. And there it still lies, but where exactly possibly nobody knows.

The Scottish people had many hard times after the days of Wallace and Bruce, but the memory of these two men was an inspiration to them. They became heroes and stories about them were handed down from father to son, told and retold many times. Sometimes these stories became exaggerated. Only later were they written down: in John Barbour's 'The Bruce' and in 'The Deeds of Sir William Wallace' by Blind Harry, which was a special favourite with generations of people. What Wallace and Bruce had fought for was freedom and so they are an inspiration to all men who love to be free.

> Ah! Freedom is a noble thing!
> Freedom makes a man to have liking;
> Freedom all *solace* to man gives;
> He lives at ease that freely lives!
> A noble heart may have none ease,
> Na elles nocht [nor anything else] that
>   may him please,
> If freedom fail; for free liking
> Is yearned over all other thing.
>
> *(John Barbour 'The Bruce')*

Things to do

1. Look out for place-names that have the following endings: *-toun* or *-ton; -rigs; -muir; -port; -gate*. What do they tell you about these places?
2. Look up an encyclopedia or 'The Dictionary of National Biography' to find out more about Michael Scot and Duns Scotus.
3. Suggest ways in which life in country and burgh is different today from what it was in the thirteenth century. Make a list of the differences under such headings as 'size and lay-out of towns'; 'ways of earning a living'; 'the inside of houses'. Have a discussion on 'Are we better off than our ancestors?'
4. Follow the chapters in this book and write a play entitled, 'The Scottish War of Independence'. The opening scene could be the last meeting of Alexander III and his council; the closing scene might be the death of Bruce.
5. Have a debate on the motion, 'That the Scottish War of Independence was not worth the time and effort'.
6. Here are some suggestions for things to draw:
   the burgh fair; a tournament; inside a merchant's house; the crowning of Bruce; the trial of Wallace; the death of Sir James Douglas in Spain.
7. You may like to try making some of these:
   a house in a farm toun, using modelling clay or small stones stuck together with clear adhesive, straw and twigs; Dirleton Castle, using polystyrene or cardboard, following the diagram in the official guide-book to the Castle; shields bearing your own design; clothes for dolls; a model of the Battle of Bannockburn, with the help of the plan on page 78, using a sand-tray and model soldiers.
8. Try to visit places associated with the events described in this book. Here are some suggestions:
   The site of the Battle of Bannockburn; the Wallace Monument at Stirling; Arbroath Abbey, where the famous Declaration was drawn up; Glasgow Cathedral; Leuchars Church in Fife and Dalmeny Church in West Lothian were all standing in the thirteenth century and so was Bothwell Castle in Lanarkshire. There are beautiful ruined abbeys at Melrose, Dryburgh, Kelso and Jedburgh.

Glossary

alcove, recess without a door
alms, gift made out of kindness
arrayed, arranged
astrology, study of the influence of stars on human affairs
bailie, leading official in a town, like an English alderman
ballads, stories told in rhyme
bannocks, flat cakes
basinet, light helmet
bereft of, without
boll, Scottish measure for weighing grain that was equal to 6 bushels
bondage, slavery
brander, Scottish gridiron or metal frame for grilling over a fire
brazil-wood, red dye-wood
brine, very salty water
burgh, borough in England
byre, cow house
carcase, dead body
cauldron, large pot
causey, causeway, raised path
cavalcade, line of people on horseback
chalder, Scottish measure for weighing that was equal to 3 cwt.
chemise, woman's skirt or shift
chute, here, trough or gutter leading down castle wall towards moat
clement, merciful, kind or gentle
coif, close-fitting cap
confiscate, take possession of
convent, monastery, now usually used only of nunneries
coulter, iron cutter on a plough
cowl, hood, close-fitting headdress
defile, gorge
diligently, carefully
diocese, area supervised by a bishop
dispose, arrange
divers, different
divot, slice of turf
ell, old measure equal to $1\frac{1}{4}$ yards
farrier, one who shoes horses
feudalism, system by which land was held on condition of service from various ranks to their superiors

flail, flat wooden stick for beating the grain from the husk of corn
flesher, butcher
girdle, Scottish griddle, flat iron plate for baking
gylfat, old Scottish vat used in brewing
hauberk, long coat of chain mail
helm, helmet
hose, here, close-fitting trousers and stockings combined
hurdle, rough sledge
in accord, unanimously, altogether
kail, (or kale), a kind of cabbage
kist, Scottish chest
laver, basin
league, old measure of length, slightly longer than a mile
lute, musical instrument with strings, shaped like half a pear
mace, metal-headed club, sometimes with spikes
madder, red dye-wood
manse, home of a minister in Scotland
Mass, celebrating the Lord's Supper, now in Roman Catholic churches
mazer, wooden cup
meal, grain ground to powder
mess, here, helping or portion of food
mortar and pestle, heavy bowl (usually stone) and stone instrument for pounding food
Mounth, Central Highlands of Scotland
muir, Scottish moor or heath
ordain, order
paid homage, promised solemnly to serve as his man
palfrey, small horse
palisade, fence of stakes
panniers, baskets
peats, blocks of moss and heather roots dug out of a bog and dried for fuel
platter, large, flat plate
portcullis, grating let down to close gateway
proffered, offered
quern, stone hand-mill
regalia, royal symbols, such as crown and sceptre
rood, crucifix
salvo, shooting together
sanctuary, refuge
schiltron, circle of spearmen facing outwards
scullion, servant for lowest kind of work
shearing-hook, Scottish sickle
sickle, sharp, curved tool for cutting corn or grass

siege-engines, machines used in besieging a town or castle
skirmish, ragged fight between small groups
sojourned, remained for a short time
solace, comfort
solar, upstairs room, originally sun-room, room that catches the
stooks, bundle of sheaves
swear allegiance, promise to be a faithful subject to a King
target, small round shield
theology, knowledge about God
till, cultivate
toft, homestead in a burgh
tolls, taxes
van, front of an army
venison, flesh of deer
victualled, stocked with supplies
wain, waggon
wainscotting, wooden boards
wimple, white linen head cloth still worn by nuns today

Further reading

BARRON, E. M., *The Scottish War of Independence.* Carruthers
BARROW, G. W. S., *Robert the Bruce.* Eyre & Spottiswoode
CRUDEN, STEWART, *The Scottish Castle.* Nelson
DICKINSON, W. C., *A New History of Scotland, vol. I.* Nelson
DUGGAN, ALFRED, *Growing up in the Thirteenth Century.* Faber
FERGUSSON, SIR JAMES, *Alexander III, King of Scotland.* Maclehose
FERGUSSON, SIR JAMES, *William Wallace, Guardian of Scotland.* Macleh
FRANKLIN, T. B., *A History of Scottish Farming.* Nelson
GRANT, I. F., *The Social and Economic Development of Scotland before 16*
Oliver & Boyd
GRANT, I. F., *Everyday Life in Old Scotland.* Allen & Unwin
LABARGE, M. W., *A Baronial Household of the Thirteenth Century.* Eyre
Spottiswoode
LINDSAY, IAN G., *The Scottish Parish Kirk,* St Andrew's Press
MACKIE, R. L., *A Short History of Scotland,* edited by Gordon Donalds
Oliver & Boyd
MACPHAIL, I. M. M., *A History of Scotland, Book I.* Arnold
SIMPSON, W. DOUGLAS, *Exploring Castles,* Routledge & Kegan Paul
SINCLAIR, C., *Thatched Houses of the Old Highlands.* Oliver & Boyd